1995 CHARLTON COIN GUIDE

34TH EDITION

**Dealer's Buying Prices For
Canadian, Newfoundland and Maritime Coinage
Canadian Medals, Tokens and Paper Money
United States and World Gold Coinage**

**W. K. Cross
Publisher**

The Charlton Press

**Toronto, Ontario
Birmingham, Michigan**

Canadian Cataloguing in Publication Data
Main Entry under title:
Charlton Coin Guide
ISSN 0706-0459
ISBN 0-88968-134-1 (34th ed.)
1. Coins, Canadian--Periodicals. 2. Coins--Prices--Periodicals.
CJ1864.C5114 737.4'4'71 C79-030323-X

Printed in Canada
in the Province of Quebec

The Charlton Press

2010 Yonge Street
Toronto, Ontario. M4S 1Z9
Tel: (416) 488-4653 Fax: (416) 488-4656

CONTENTS

Introduction 4
Coins of Canada:
- Nova Scotia 10
- Prince Edward Island 10
- New Brunswick 10
- Newfoundland 11
- Province of Canada 15
- Dominion of Canada 16

Collectors Issues 32
Olympic Coins 37
Aviation Coins 43
Gold Coins:
- $100 45
- $200 46

Maple Leaf Bullion Coins 48
Proof Platinum Coins 49
Paper Money of Canada:
- Province of Canada 50
- Dominion of Canada 50
- Bank of Canada 55

Colonial Coins and Tokens:
- Newfoundland 66
- Prince Edward Island 67
- Nova Scotia 69
- New Brunswick 72
- Lower Canada 73
- Wellington Tokens 76
- Upper Canada Tokens 77
- Province of Canada 78

Anonymous and Miscellaneous 79
Canadian Medals 81
Coins of the United States 87
World Gold Coins 101
Appendix - Gold and Silver Bullion Values 104

INDEX OF ADVERTISERS

Albern Coins and Foreign Exchange . . 7
Bob Armstrong Coins 46
Canadian Association of Numismatic Dealers 106
Chantou International 111
Charlton Press 110
Gatewest 4
Guntram Weisbrich 8
Imperial Coin Company 109
Jeffrey Hoare Auctions Inc. 107
K. L. Coin Co. 112
Lincoln Heights Coin & Stamp 108
London Coin Centre 109
Marc Verret Numismatics 36
Proof Positive Coins 5
Provincial Coin Co. Ltd. 3
Torex 107

INTRODUCTION

It is more difficult to obtain old coins in circulation, much more so than it was twenty years ago. For the most part silver no longer circulates since its bullion value now exceeds its face value. Generally speaking, the only pre-1968 coins in circulation are one-cent and five-cent pieces, and these seldom pre-date 1953. Older coins must now be purchased through dealers.

BUYING AND SELLING PRICES

Buying prices are what dealers pay for coins. Selling prices are what dealers charge for coins. Generally, dealers will pay 40% to 60% of their selling price. It should be remembered, all dealers will pay according to their needs. They will pay well for what they need immediately, but for those coins for which there is no demand, even if they have a high retail value, they will offer substantially less.

The prices shown in this book represent averages or estimates of buying prices, and should serve as a guide in negotiating fair prices when buying or selling. Also a clearer idea of what coins are in demand by collectors and dealers can be developed by studying the guide.

Coins should not be mailed for appraisal unless a written response to an inquiry is received from the dealer. If coins are mailed, then they should be sent by registered mail, insured, accompanied by a list of the coins sent, and with a complete return address and return postage.

HANDLING AND CLEANING COINS

Coins should be handled by the edges only. Avoid touching the surfaces. Many collectors have found too late that fingerprints cannot be removed from coins or other metal valuables. Proof and Specimen quality coins must be handled with extra care since their high lustre is very fragile.

Inevitably, the question of whether to clean coins or not will arise. Probably the best course to follow is, when in doubt - don't, until you have contacted an experienced collector or dealer.

The tarnish on silver coins can be removed, but it will not necessarily raise the value. If the tarnish is very thick, then its removal could leave the coin looking much worse.

Nickel coins seldom require cleaning, and only soap and water are safe since nickel is a fairly active metal. Copper and bronze should not be cleaned by anyone who is not knowledgeable in the chemical properties of these metals and their alloys.

Whatever the metal, abrasives must never be used. There are many polishes on the market which are designed for silverware, copper and brass. These must not be used with coins. The results are disastrous

HANDLING AND CLEANING PAPER MONEY

Inexperienced collectors should always use great care when handling notes. Notes should be handled as little as possible, since oil and perspiration from one's skin can damage and devalue a note. Care should be taken to ensure that unfolded or uncreased notes remain so, and that even marginal tears or abrasions are avoided. Under no circumstances should one ever wash or otherwise try to clean a note since it is likely that the note's value will be considerably reduced. The same is true for ironing or pressing. It should be avoided.

MINT MARKS

A mint mark is a letter stamped on a coin to designate the mint that produced the coins.

Canadian decimal coinage issued prior to 1908 was struck at either the Tower Mint, London, in which case it had no mint mark, or at the Heaton Mint in Birmingham. The Birmingham coins have a small "H" as a mint mark. Since 1908 all Canadian coins have been struck at the Ottawa or Winnipeg Mints, with no mint marks, except the Canadian sovereigns which were identified by a small "C" above the date.

Newfoundland's coinage was struck at either London, Birmingham, or Ottawa. The Tower Mint coins had no marks, the Birmingham coins had an "H", and the Ottawa coins had a "C", except for the 1940 and 1942 cent pieces.

New Brunswick's and Nova Scotia's coinage had no mint marks because it was struck at the Tower Mint.

Prince Edward Island's coinage was struck at Birmingham but no mint mark was used because the dies were supplied by the Tower Mint.

COINS OF CANADA

NOVA SCOTIA

VICTORIA 1861 - 1864

Date and Denomination	Buying Price
1861 half cent	2.00
1864 half cent	2.00
1861 one cent	1.25
1862 one cent	11.00
1864 one cent	1.25

PRINCE EDWARD ISLAND

VICTORIA 1871

Date and Denomination	Buying Price
1871 one cent	1.00

IMPORTANT

Buying prices are listed for coins graded VG or better. Bent, damaged or badly worn coins are not collectable and bring no premium value.

NEW BRUNSWICK

VICTORIA 1861 - 1864

Date and Denomination	Buying Price
1861 half cent	30.00
1861 one cent	1.25
1864 one cent	1.25
1862 five cents	18.00
1864 five cents	18.00
1862 ten cents	18.00
1864 ten cents	18.00
1862 twenty cents	8.00
1864 twenty cents	8.00

IMPORTANT

Do not clean your coins. Coins should be handled carefully. Only experts should consider cleaning. If you are not an expert the results can be disastrous.

NEWFOUNDLAND

LARGE CENTS

Wide O

Narrow O

VICTORIA 1865 - 1896

Date and Mint Mark	Description	Buying Price
1865		1.25
1872H		1.25
1873		1.25
1876H		1.25
1880	Wide O	1.25
1880	Narrow O	35.00
1885		6.00
1888		6.00
1890		1.25
1894		1.25
1896		1.25

EDWARD VII 1904 - 1909

Date and Mint Mark	Description	Buying Price
1904H		2.50
1907		.75
1909		.75

GEORGE V 1913 - 1936

Date and Mint Mark	Description	Buying Price
1913		.25
1917C		.25
1919C		.25
1920C		.25
1929		.25
1936		.25

SMALL CENTS

GEORGE VI 1938 - 1948

Date and Mint Mark	Description	Buying Price
1938		.15
1940		.15
1940	Re-engraved Date	10.00
1941C		.15
1942		.15
1943C		.15
1944C		.15
1947C		.15

FIVE CENTS

VICTORIA 1865 - 1896

Date and Mint Mark	Description	Buying Price
1865		12.00
1870		14.00
1872H		12.00
1873		14.00

Date and Mint Mark	Description	Buying Price
1873H		450.00
1876H		45.00
1880		8.00
1881		6.00
1882H		5.00
1885		50.00
1888		9.00
1890		2.50
1894		2.50
1896		1.00

EDWARD VII 1903 - 1908

Date and Mint Mark	Description	Buying Price
1903		1.00
1904H		1.00
1908		1.00

GEORGE V 1912 - 1929

Date and Mint Mark	Description	Buying Price
1912		.75
1917C		.75
1919C		.75
1929		.75

GEORGE VI 1938 - 1947

Date and Mint Mark	Description	Buying Price
1938		.50
1940C		.50
1941C		.50
1942C		.50
1943C		.50
1944C		.50
1945C		.50
1946C		125.00
1947C		.50

TEN CENTS

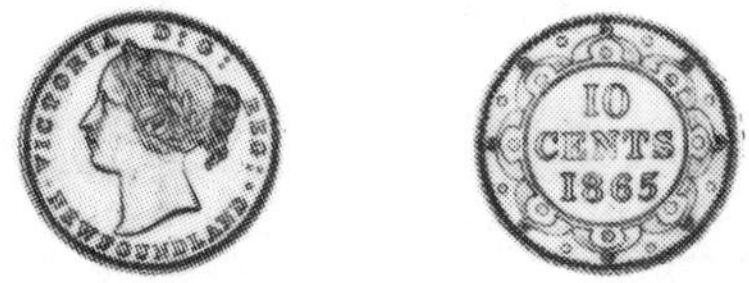

VICTORIA 1865 - 1896

Date and Mint Mark	Description	Buying Price
1865		6.00
1870		75.00
1872H		6.00
1873		6.00
1876H		9.00
1880		9.00
1882H		6.00
1885		30.00
1888		5.00
1890		1.75
1894		1.75
1896		1.50

EDWARD VII 1903 - 1904

Date and Mint Mark	Description	Buying Price
1903		.50
1904H		.50

GEORGE V 1912 -1919

Date and Mint Mark	Description	Buying Price
1912		.35
1917C		.35
1919C		.35

IMPORTANT

Buying prices are listed for coins graded VG or better. Bent, damaged or badly worn coins are not collectable and bring no premium value.

GEORGE VI 1938 - 1947

Date and Mint Mark	Description	Buying Price
1938		.35
1940		.35
1941C		.35
1942C		.35
1943C		.35
1944C		.35
1945C		.35
1946C		.35
1947C		.35

TWENTY CENTS

VICTORIA 1865 - 1900

Date and Mint Mark	Description	Buying Price
1865		6.00
1870		6.00
1872H		4.00
1873		4.00
1876H		5.00
1880		6.00
1881		2.00
1882H		1.50
1885		3.00
1888		1.50
1890		1.50
1894		1.50
1896		.75
1899		.75
1900		.75

IMPORTANT

Mint marks are a letter stamped on a coin to designate the mint that produced the coin. The Canadian Mint used the letter "C", while the Heaton Mint in England used the letter "H".

EDWARD VII 1904

Date and Mint Mark	Description	Buying Price
1904H		4.00

GEORGE V 1912

Date and Mint Mark	Description	Buying Price
1912		.70

TWENTY-FIVE CENTS

GEORGE V 1917 - 1919

Date and Mint Mark	Description	Buying Price
1917C		.90
1919C		.90

IMPORTANT

Buying prices are listed for coins graded VG or better. Bent, damaged or badly worn coins are not collectable and bring no premium.

FIFTY CENTS

VICTORIA 1870 - 1900

Date and Mint Mark	Description	Buying Price
1870		5.00
1872H		5.00
1873		10.00
1874		5.00
1876H		10.00
1880		10.00
1881		5.00
1882H		4.00
1885		5.00
1888		6.00
1894		1.75
1896		1.75
1898		1.75
1899		1.75
1900		1.75

EDWARD VII 1904 - 1909

Date and Mint Mark	Description	Buying Price
1904H		1.75
1907		1.75
1908		1.75
1909		1.75

GEORGE V 1911 - 1919

Date and Mint Mark	Description	Buying Price
1911		1.75
1917C		1.75
1918C		1.75
1919C		1.75

TWO DOLLARS GOLD

VICTORIA 1865 - 1888

Date and Mint Mark	Description	Buying Price
1865		125.00
1870		135.00
1872		175.00
1880		600.00
1881		120.00
1882H		120.00
1885		120.00
1888		120.00

PROVINCE OF CANADA

LARGE CENTS

VICTORIA 1858 - 1859

Date and Mint Mark	Description	Buying Price
1858		30.00
1859		1.00
1859	W/9 over 8	12.00

FIVE CENTS

Large Date

Small Date

VICTORIA 1858

Date and Mint Mark	Description	Buying Price
1858	Small Date	6.00
1858	Large Date	65.00

IMPORTANT

Mint marks are a letter stamped on a coin to designate the mint that produced the coin. The Canadian Mint used the letter "C", while the Heaton Mint in England used the letter "H".

TEN CENTS

VICTORIA 1858

Date and Mint Mark	Description	Buying Price
1858		7.50

TWENTY CENTS

VICTORIA 1858

Date and Mint Mark	Description	Buying Price
1858		30.00

IMPORTANT

The buying prices for silver coins are based on their intrinsic value. All issues from 1902 to 1968 are priced at the market value for $5.50 (Can. Funds) silver. Conditions play an important part in the buying price for coins between 1902 and 1936. Higher or lower silver prices will change the listed values.

IMPORTANT

Buying prices are listed for coins graded VG or better. Bent, damaged or badly worn coins are not collectable and bring no premium value.

DOMINION OF CANADA

LARGE CENTS

Large Date, Large Leaves

Small Date, Small Leaves

VICTORIA 1876 - 1901

Date and Mint Mark	Description	Buying Price
1876H		1.00
1881H		1.00
1882H		1.00
1884		1.00
1886		1.00
1887		1.00
1888		1.00
1890H		1.50
1891	Large Leaves, Large Date	1.50
1891	Large Leaves, Small Date	30.00
1891	Small Leaves, Small Date	20.00
1892		1.00
1893		1.00
1894		1.00
1895		1.25
1896		1.00
1897		1.00
1898H		1.00
1899		1.00
1900		1.25
1900H		1.00
1901		1.00

Large cents were not issued for the years omitted in this listing.

EDWARD VII 1902 - 1910

Date and Mint Mark	Description	Buying Price
1902		.50
1903		.50
1904		.50
1905		.50
1906		.50
1907		.50
1907H		2.00
1908		.50
1909		.50
1910		.50

GEORGE V 1911 - 1920

Date and Mint Mark	Description	Buying Price
1911		.25
1912		.25
1913		.25
1914		.25
1915		.25
1916		.25
1917		.25
1918		.25
1919		.25
1920		.25

IMPORTANT

Buying prices are listed for coins graded VG or better. Bent, damaged or badly worn coins are not collectable and bring no premium value.

SMALL CENTS

GEORGE V 1920 - 1936

Date and Mint Mark	Description	Buying Price
1920		.05
1921		.05
1922		6.00
1923		11.00
1924		3.00
1925		9.00
1926		.50
1927		.15
1928		.05
1929		.05
1930		.30
1931		.10
1932 to 1936		.05

1937 Obverse 1937 Reverse

1947 Maple Leaf

GEORGE VI 1937 - 1952

Date and Mint Mark	Description	Buying Price
1937 to 1947		.01
1947	Maple Leaf	.01

In 1948 "ET IND:IMP." ceased to appear on the coinage.

Date and Mint Mark	Description	Buying Price
1948 to 1952		.01

No Shoulder Fold

Shoulder Fold

ELIZABETH II 1953 To date

Date and Mint Mark	Description	Buying Price
1953	NSF	.01
1953	SF	.05
1954		.01
1954		.01
1955		.01
1955	NSF	50.00
1956 to 1964		.01

Mature Head-Round Centennial

Date and Mint Mark	Description	Buying Price
1965 to 1966 Mature Head		.01
1967	Centennial	.01
1968 to 1981		.01

Mature Head Double Date
12 Sided Crowned Head

Date and Mint Mark	Description	Buying Price
1982 to 1989	Mature Head	.01
1990 to 1991	Crowned Head	.01
1992	Double Date	.01

Date and Mint Mark	Description	Buying Price
1993 to 1995		.01

FIVE CENTS SILVER

1900 Small Date

1900 Large Date

Plain 4

Crosslet 4

VICTORIA 1870 - 1901

Date and Mint Mark	Description	Buying Price
1870		3.50
1871		3.50
1872H		2.50
1874H	Plain 4	7.00
1874H	Crosslet 4	4.50
1875H	Large Date	60.00
1875H	Small Date	50.00
1880H		1.50
1881H		1.50
1882H		1.50
1883H		4.50
1884		40.00
1885		2.50
1886		1.50
1887		4.50
1888		1.50
1889		7.00
1890H		1.50
1891		1.50
1892		1.50
1893		1.50
1894		4.50
1896		1.50
1897		1.50
1898		3.50
1899		1.50
1900	Large Date	6.00
1900	Small Date	1.50
1901		1.50

Small H

Large H

EDWARD VII 1902 - 1910

Date and Mint Mark	Description	Buying Price
1902	Plain	1.00
1902	Large H	1.00
1902	Small H	3.50
1903		1.50
1903H		1.00
1904		1.00
1905		1.00
1906		1.00
1907		1.00
1908		1.50
1909		1.00
1910		1.00

GEORGE V 1911 - 1921

Date and Mint Mark	Description	Buying Price
1911		.50
1912		.50
1913		.50
1914		.50
1915		2.50
1916		.50
1917		.50
1918		.50
1919		.50
1920		.50
1921		800.00

FIVE CENTS NICKEL

Near 6

Far 6

GEORGE V 1922 - 1936

Date and Mint Mark	Description	Buying Price
1922 to 1924		.07
1925		15.00
1926	Near 6	.25
1926	Far 6	45.00
1927 to 1936		.07

Tombac Beaver

Tombac "V"

1947 Maple Leaf

GEORGE VI 1937 - 1952

Date and Mint Mark	Description	Buying Price
1937	Dot	.05
1938 to 1941		.05
1942	Nickel	.05
1942	Tombac Beaver	.15
1943	Tombac V	.07
1944 to 1945	Steel V	.05
1946 to 1947		.05
1947	Maple Leaf	.05

In 1948 "ET IND:IMP." ceased to appear on the coinage.

Geo. VI Obverse

Beaver

1951 Comm.

1951 High Relief

Date and Mint Mark	Description	Buying Price
1948 to 1951		.05
1951	Commemorative	.05
1951	High Relief	100.00
1952		.05

1953/64 Young Head - Beaver

1965/89 Mature Head - Centennial

1990/92 Crowned Head - Double Date

ELIZABETH II 1953 to date

Date and Mint Mark	Description	Buying Price
1953 to 1964	Young Head	.05
1965 to 1966	Mature Head	.05
1967	Centennial	.05
1968 to 1989	Mature Head	.05
1990 to 1991	Crowned Head	.05
1992	Double Date	.05

Date and Mint Mark	Description	Buying Price
1993 to 1995		.05

TEN CENTS

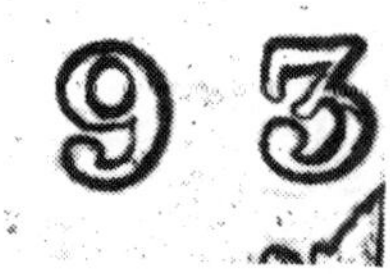

Flat Top 3

Round Top 3

VICTORIA 1870 - 1901

Date and Mint Mark	Description	Buying Price
1870		4.50
1871		5.00
1871H		6.00
1872H		35.00
1874H		3.00
1875H		100.00
1880H		3.00
1881H		3.00
1882H		3.00
1883H		8.50
1884		75.00
1885		6.00
1886		4.50
1887		7.00
1888		3.00
1889		200.00
1890H		3.50
1891		3.50
1892		3.00
1893	Flat Top 3	5.00
1893	Round Top 3	250.00
1894		3.50
1896		3.00
1898		3.00
1899		3.00
1900		2.50
1901		2.50

EDWARD VII 1902 - 1910

Date and Mint Mark	Description	Buying Price
1902		1.00
1902H		1.00
1903		3.00
1903H		1.00
1904		1.00
1905		1.00
1906		1.00
1907		1.00
1908		1.00
1909		1.00
1910		1.00

Small Leaves

Broad Leaves

GEORGE V 1911 - 1936

Date and Mint Mark	Description	Buying Price
1911		2.50
1912		.35
1913	Broad Leaves	50.00
1913	Small Leaves	.35
1914 to 1936		.35

GEORGE VI 1937 - 1952

Date and Mint Mark	Description	Buying Price
1937 to 1947		.35
1947	Maple Leaf	.35

In 1948 "ET IND:IMP." ceased to appear on coinage.

Date and Mint Mark	Description	Buying Price
1948		.75
1949 to 1952		.35

1953/64 Young Head

Blue Nose

1965/89 Mature Head

Centennial Reverse

1991/92 Crowned Head

Double Date Reverse

1969 Small Date

1969 Large Date

ELIZABETH II 1952 to date

Date and Mint Mark	Description	Buying Price
1953 to 1964	Young Head	.35
1965 to 1966	Mature Head	.35
1967	Centennial	.25
1968	.500 Fine Silver	.15
1968	Nickel	.10
1969	Large Date	3,000.00
1969	Small Date	.10
1970 to 1989	Mature Head	.10
1990 to 1991	Crowned Head	.10
1992	Double Date	.10

Date and Mint Mark	Description	Buying Price
1993 to 1995		.10

TWENTY-FIVE CENTS

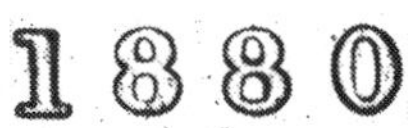

Narrow O

Wide O

VICTORIA 1870 - 1901

Date and Mint Mark	Description	Buying Price
1870		3.50
1871		4.50
1871H		6.00
1872H		3.00
1874H		3.00
1875H		150.00
1880H	Narrow O	12.00
1880H	Wide O	50.00
1881H		3.50
1882H		4.50
1883H		3.50
1885		40.00
1886		3.50
1887		40.00
1888		4.50
1889		50.00
1890H		6.00
1891		20.00
1892		3.50
1893		40.00
1894		4.50
1899		3.00
1900		2.00
1901		3.00

EDWARD VII 1902 - 1910

Date and Mint Mark	Description	Buying Price
1902		1.00
1902H		1.00
1903		1.00
1904		4.00
1905		1.00
1906		1.00
1907		1.00
1908		1.00
1909		1.00
1910		1.00

GEORGE V 1911- 1936

Date and Mint Mark	Description	Buying Price
1911		3.00
1912 to 1914		1.00
1915		4.50
1916 to 1920		1.00
1921		3.50
1927		8.00
1928 to 1936		1.00
1936	Dot	15.00

GEORGE VI 1937 - 1952

Date and Mint Mark	Description	Buying Price
1937 to 1947		.90
1947	Maple Leaf	.90

In 1948 "ET IND"IMP." ceased to appear on the coinage.

Date and Mint Mark	Description	Buying Price
1948 to 1952		.90

1953/64 Young Head

Caribou

1965/1972 Mature Head
Large Bust

Centennial

ELIZABETH II 1953 to date

Date and Mint Mark	Description	Buying Price
1953	Large Date	.90
1953	Small Date	.90
1954 to 1964	Young Head	.90
1965 to 1966	Mature Head	.25
1967	Centennial	.35
1968	.500 Fine Silver	.30
1968 to 1972	Nickel	.25

IMPORTANT

Do not clean your coins. Coins should be handled carefully. Only experts should consider cleaning. If you are not an expert the results can be disastrous.

1973 Large Bust
132 Obverse Beads
Near Rim

1973 Small Bust
120 Obverse Beads
Far from Rim

RCMP

Caribou

1974/89 Mature Head
Small Beads

1990/91 Crowned Head

Date and Mint Mark	Description	Buying Price
1973	Small Bust	.25
1973	Large Bust	30.00
1974 to 1989	Mature Head Head	.25
1990 to 1991	Crowned Head	.25

CANADA 125 ANNIVERSARY

Issued in 1992 to commemorate Canada's 125th birthday. The twelve different quarters represent images from the ten provinces and two territories. The composition is nickel.

Common
Obverse

New Brunswick

Northwest
Territories

Newfoundland

Manitoba

Yukon

Alberta

Prince Edward Island

Ontario

Nova Scotia

Quebec

Saskatchewan

British Columbia

Date and Mint Mark	Description	Buying Price
1992	New Brunswick	.25
1992	Northwest Territories	.25
1992	Newfoundland	.25
1992	Manitoba	.25
1992	Yukon	.25
1992	Alberta	.25
1992	Prince Edward Island	.25
1992	Ontario	.25
1992	Nova Scotia	.25
1992	Quebec	.25
1992	Saskatchewan	.25
1992	British Columbia	.25

PROOF SILVER SET

Issued by the Mint in 1992. The silver twenty-five cent coins were sold singly and in sets. The 13 coins are 12 - 25¢ coins and a dollar coin, the set is housed in a blue presentation box.

Buying Prices: Singly: $5.00 Set: $60.00

Date and Mint Mark	Description	Buying Price
1993 to Date	Crowned Head	.25

IMPORTANT

Buyng prices are listed for coins graded VG or better. Bent, damaged or badly worn coins are not collectable and bring no premium value.

FIFTY CENTS

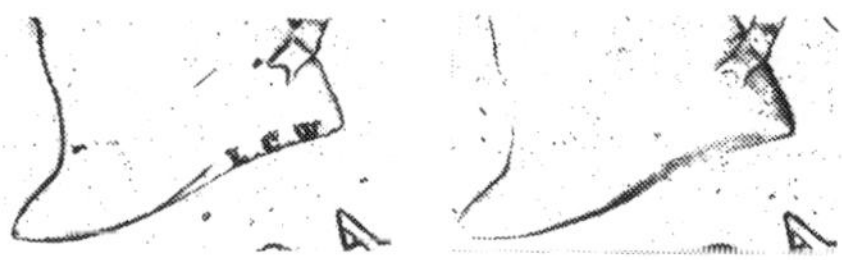

L.C.W. No L.C.W.

VICTORIA 1870 - 1901

Date and Mint Mark	Description	Buying Price
1870	Without L.C.W.	300.00
1870	With L.C.W.	16.00
1871		17.00
1871H		27.00
1872H		16.00
1881H		16.00
1888		37.00
1890H		400.00
1892		17.00
1894		125.00
1898		15.00
1899		25.00
1900		12.00
1901		12.00

EDWARD VII 1902 - 1910

Date and Mint Mark	Description	Buying Price
1902		7.00
1903H		6.00
1904		50.00
1905		60.00

Date and Mint Mark	Description	Buying Price
1906		6.00
1907		4.50
1908		1.75
1909		1.75
1910		1.75

GEORGE V 1911 - 1936

Date and Mint Mark	Description	Buying Price
1911 to 1920		1.75
1921*		5,000.00
1929		1.75
1931		1.75
1932		16.00
1934		6.00
1936		5.00

*Majority were melted down, approximately 75 are known. Beware of altered date.

GEORGE VI 1937 - 1952

Date and Mint Mark	Description	Buying Price
1937 to 1946		1.75

IMPORTANT

Buying prices are listed for coins graded VG or better. Bent, damaged or badly worn coins are not collectable and bring no premium value.

Maple Leaf | No Maple Leaf

1947 Straight "7"

Maple Leaf | No Maple Leaf

1947 Curved "7"

Date and Mint Mark	Description	Buying Price
1947	Straight "7"	1.75
1947	Curved "7"	1.75
1947	M.L., Straight "7"	9.00
1947	M.L., Curved "7"	600.00

In 1948 "ET IND:IMP." ceased to appear on the coinage

Date and Mint Mark	Description	Buying Price
1948		20.00
1949 to 1952		1.75

IMPORTANT

Do not clean your coins. Coins should be handled carefully. Only experts should consider cleaning. If you are not an expert the results can be disastrous.

No Shoulder Fold

Shoulder Fold

Small Date

Large Date

ELIZABETH II 1953 to date

Date and Mint Mark	Description	Buying Price
1953	SD, NSF	1.75
1953	LD, NSF	2.50
1953	LD, SF	1.75
1954 to 1964		1.75

Date and Mint Mark	Description	Buying Price
1965 to 1966		1.75
1967	Centennial	2.00

Date and Mint Mark	Description	Buying Price
1968 to 1989	Mature Head	.50

Date and Mint Mark	Description	Buying Price
1990 to 1991	Crowned Head	.50

Date and Mint Mark	Description	Buying Price
1992	1867-1992	.50

Date and Mint Mark	Description	Buying Price
1993 to Date	Crowned Head	.50

SILVER DOLLARS

1935 Obverse

1936 Obverse

1937 to 1947 Obverse

1935 Reverse

1939 Parliament

1949 Newfoundland

1947 Blunt 7

1947 Pointed 7

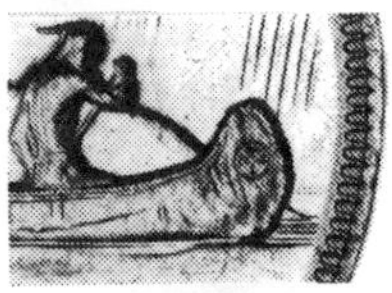

1952
Waterlines

1952
No Waterlines

1947 Maple Leaf

GEORGE V 1935 - 1936

Date and Mint Mark	Description	Buying Price
1935	Silver Jubilee	20.00
1936	Voyageur	10.00

GEORGE VI 1937 - 1952

Date and Mint Mark	Description	Buying Price
1937	Voyageur	10.00
1938	Voyageur	25.00
1939	Royal Visit	5.00
1945	Voyageur	75.00
1946	Voyageur	15.00
1947	Blunt 7	40.00
1947	Pointed 7	65.00
1947	Maple Leaf	100.00
1948	Dei Gratia	500.00
1949	Newfoundland	10.00
1950	Voyageur	6.00
1950	Arnprior	5.00
1951	Voyageur	5.00
1951	Arnprior	20.00
1952	Waterlines	5.00
1952	No Waterlines	5.00

Arnprior dollars are known to exist in the years 1950, 1951 and 1955. Other years may contain Arnprior varieties but are unknown at the present time.

Obverse

1953 Reverse

1964 Charlottetown

1958 British Columbia

1965 Obverse

1967 Centennial

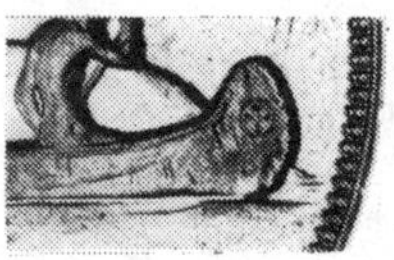

1955 No Water Lines

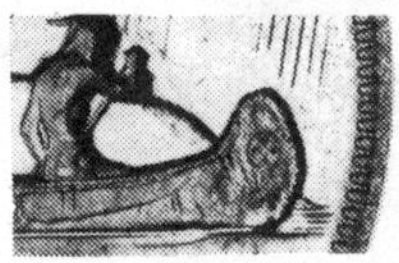

1955 2 1/2 Waterlines

ELIZABETH II 1953 to date

Date and Mint Mark	Description	Buying Price
1953	Voyageur	3.50
1954	Voyageur	3.50
1955	Voyageur	3.50
1955 Arnprior	Voyageur	40.00
1956	Voyageur	3.50
1957	Voyageur	3.50
1957 Arnprior	One Waterline	3.50
1958	British Columbia	3.50
1959	Voyageur	3.50
1960	Voyageur	3.50
1961	Voyageur	3.50
1962	Voyageur	3.50
1963	Voyageur	3.50
1964	Charlottetown	3.50
1965	Voyageur	3.50
1966	Voyageur	3.50
1967	Centennial	3.50

IMPORTANT

Do not clean your coins. Coins should be handled carefully. Only experts should consider cleaning. If you are not an expert the results can be disastrous.

IMPORTANT

The silver dollar buying prices are for problem free coins in very fine condition. Damaged coins will bring lower prices

NICKEL DOLLARS

1968 to 1987 Obverse

Reverse

Manitoba

British Columbia

Prince Edward Island

Winnipeg

Constitution

Jacques Cartier

Date and Mint Mark	Description	Buying Price
1968	Voyageur	1.00
1969	Voyageur	1.00
1970	Manitoba	1.00
1971	British Columbia	1.00
1972	Voyageur	1.00
1973	P.E.I.	1.00
1974	Winnipeg	1.00
1975 to 1981	Voyageur	1.00
1982	Constitution	1.00
1983	Voyageur	1.00
1984	Jacques Cartier	1.00
1985	Voyageur	1.00
1986	Voyageur	1.00
1987	Voyageur	1.00

Date and Mint Mark	Description	Buying Price
1987 to 1989	Loon	1.00

Date and Mint Mark	Description	Buying Price
1990 to 1991	Loon	1.00

CANADA 125

Issued to commemorate the 125th birthday of Canada.

Date and Mint Mark	Description	Buying Price
1992	Canada 125	1.00

Date and Mint Mark	Description	Buying Price
1992	Double Date	1.00
1993 to 1994	Loon	1.00

Date and Mint Mark	Description	Buying Price
1994	Memorial	1.00

GOLD COINS

SOVEREIGNS

EDWARD VII 1908 - 1910

Date and Mint Mark	Description	Buying Price
1908C		1000.00
1909C		150.00
1910C		140.00

GEORGE V 1911 - 1919

Date and Mint Mark	Description	Buying Price
1911C		125.00
1913C		300.00
1914C		150.00
1916C		5,000.00
1917C		125.00
1918C		125.00
1919C		125.00

FIVE DOLLARS

GEORGE V 1912 - 1914

Date and Mint Mark	Description	Buying Price
1912		150.00
1913		150.00
1914		250.00

TEN DOLLARS

GEORGE V 1912 - 1914

Date and Mint Mark	Description	Buying Price
1912		300.00
1913		300.00
1914		310.00

TWENTY DOLLARS

ELIZABETH II 1953 to date

Date and Mint Mark	Description	Buying Price
1967	Centennial	265.00
1967	Complete Set	275.00

IMPORTANT

Do not clean your coins. Coins should be handled carefully. Only experts should consider cleaning. If you are not an expert the results can be disastrous.

COLLECTORS ISSUES

The Numismatic department of the Royal Canadian Mint issued specially struck and packaged coins starting in 1954. The coins were issued for collectors and as a result are of high quality. The dealer buying prices listed below are for single coins and sets in their original packaging and condition. Coins or sets which have been mishandled or damaged are discounted from the prices listed. Beginning in 1971 the Numismatic Department of the Royal Canadian Mint issued silver dollars for collectors in two conditions, proof and uncirculated. Proof condition dollars were issued in black leatherette boxes while uncirculated dollars were issued in a clear plastic container.

SILVER PROOF-LIKE DOLLARS

Date	Description	Buying Price	Date	Description	Buying Price
1954	Voyageur	100.00	1959	Voyageur	10.00
1955	Voyageur	80.00	1960	Voyageur	8.00
1955	Arnprior	100.00	1961	Voyageur	6.00
1956	Voyageur	50.00	1962	Voyageur	3.50
1957	Voyageur	20.00	1963	Voyageur	3.50
1958	British Columbia	20.00	1964	Charlottetown	3.50

CASED NICKEL DOLLARS

Manitoba

British Columbia

Prince Edward Island

Winnipeg

Constitution

Jacques Cartier

Date	Description	Buying Price	Date	Description	Buying Price
1970	Manitoba	1.00	1975	Voyageur	1.00
1971	British Columbia	1.00	1976	Voyageur	1.00
1972	Voyageur	1.00	1982	Constitution	3.00
1973	Prince Edward Island	1.00	1984	Jacques Cartier	3.00
1974	Winnipeg	1.00	1987	Loon	4.00

CASED SILVER DOLLARS

Common Obverse

1971 British Columbia

1973 R.C.M.P

1974 Winnipeg

1975 Calgary

1976 Parliament

1977 Jubilee

1978 Commonwealth

1979 Griffon

Date	Description	Buying Price
1971	British Columbia	8.00
1972	Voyageur	4.00
1973	R.C.M.P.	7.00
1974	Winnipeg	7.00
1975	Calgary Stampede	5.00

Date	Description	Buying Price
1976	Library of Parliament	12.00
1977	Jubilee	7.00
1978	Commonwealth Games	7.00
1979	Griffon	15.00

1980 Arctic Territories

1981 Trans Canada

1982 Regina

1983 University Games

1984 Toronto

1985 National Parks

1986 Vancouver

1987 Davis Strait

1988 Ironworks

Date	Description	Buying Price
1980	Arctic Territories	30.00
1981	Trans Canada (PF)	18.00
1981	Trans Canada (UNC)	15.00
1982	Regina (PF)	5.00
1982	Regina (UNC)	15.00
1983	University Games (PF)	7.00
1983	University Games (UNC)	8.00
1984	Toronto (PF)	6.00
1984	Toronto (UNC)	18.00
1985	National Parks (PF)	6.00
1985	National Parks (UNC)	15.00
1986	Vancouver (PF)	7.00
1986	Vancouver (UNC)	25.00
1987	Davis Strait (PF)	12.00
1987	Davis Strait (UNC)	15.00
1988	Ironworks (PF)	25.00
1988	Ironworks (UNC)	25.00

1989 MacKenzie River

Common Obverse

1990 Henry Kelsey

1991 Frontenac

1992 Stagecoach

1993 Hockey

1994 Royal Canadian Mounted Police

Date	Description	Buying Price
1989	MacKenzie River (PF)	25.00
1989	MacKenzie River (UNC)	15.00
1990	Henry Kelsey (PF)	15.00
1990	Henry Kelsey (UNC)	10.00
1991	Frontenac (PF)	15.00
1991	Frontenac (UNC)	10.00

Date	Description	Buying Price
1992	Stagecoach (PF)	15.00
1992	Stagecoach (UNC)	10.00
1993	Hockey (PF)	15.00
1993	Hockey (UNC)	10.00
1994	RCMP (PF)	15.00
1994	RCMP (UNC)	10.00
1995	Proof	12.00
1995	Uncirculated	15.00

SILVER PROOF-LIKE SETS

Date	Description	Buying Price
1954	Voyageur	200.00
1955	Voyageur	125.00
1955	Arnprior	175.00
1956	Voyageur	80.00
1957	Voyageur	40.00
1958	British Columbia	30.00
1959	Voyageur	18.00
1960	Voyageur	11.00
1961	Voyageur	10.00
1962	Voyageur	6.50
1963	Voyageur	6.50
1964	Charlottetown	6.50
1965	Voyageur	6.50
1966	Voyageur	6.50
1967	Centennial	10.00

NICKEL PROOF-LIKE SETS

Date	Description	Buying Price
1968	Voyageur	2.00
1969	Voyageur	2.00
1970	Manitoba	2.50
1971	British Columbia	2.25
1972	Voyageur	2.25
1973	R.C.M.P., Small Bust	2.25
1973	R.C.M.P., Large Bust	75.00
1974	Winnipeg	2.50
1975	Voyageur	2.50
1976	Voyageur	3.00
1977	Voyageur	2.50
1978	Voyageur	2.50
1979	Voyageur	2.50
1980	Voyageur	3.50
1981	Voyageur	3.50
1982	Voyageur	3.00
1983	Voyageur	5.00
1984	Voyageur	5.00
1985	Voyageur	5.00
1986	Voyageur	9.00
1987	Voyageur	5.00
1988	Loon	5.00
1989	Loon	9.00
1990	Loon	8.00
1991	Loon	20.00
1992	Loon	10.00
1993	Loon	5.00
1994	Loon	5.00
1995	Loon	5.00

SPECIMEN SETS

Issued by the Royal Canadian Mint starting in 1981 and continuing to date, contains 1-cent to the nickel dollar (6 coins).

Date	Description	Buying Price
1981	Voyageur	3.00
1982	Voyageur	3.00
1983	Voyageur	3.50
1984	Voyageur	3.50
1985	Voyageur	3.50
1986	Voyageur	4.00
1987	Voyageur	4.00
1988	Loon	5.00
1989	Loon	8.00
1990	Loon	8.00
1991	Loon	20.00
1992	Loon	9.00
1993	Loon	6.00
1994	Loon	6.00
1995	Loon	6.00

PRESTIGE PROOF SETS

Issued by the Royal Canadian Mint in 1971 and continuing to date, contains 1-cent to the nickel dollar plus the silver dollar of that year (7 coins).

Date	Description	Buying Price
1971	British Columbia	9.00
1972	Voyageur	6.00
1973	R.C.M.P. Small Bust	9.00
1973	R.C.M.P. Large Bust	100.00
1974	Winnipeg	10.00
1975	Calgary	7.00
1976	Parliament	15.00
1977	Jubilee	10.00
1978	Commonwealth Games	10.00
1979	Griffon	18.00
1980	Arctic Territories	32.00
1981	Trans Canada	19.00
1982	Regina	6.50
1983	University Games	10.00
1984	Toronto	7.00
1985	National Parks	7.00
1986	Vancouver	9.00
1987	Davis Straits	14.00
1988	Ironworks	25.00
1989	MacKenzie River	25.00
1990	Henry Kelsey	25.00
1991	Frontenac	75.00
1992	Stagecoach	25.00

PRESTIGE PROOF SETS CONT'D

Date	Description	Buying Price
1994	RCMP	25.00
1995	N/A	25.00
1993	Hockey	25.00

CUSTOM SETS

These sets were issued by the Royal Canadian Mint between 1971 and 1980. They contain seven coins, the 1-cent to the nickel dollar plus an extra cent.

Date	Description	Buying Price
1971 to 1980		2.00

SPECIMEN SETS

Sets of Specimen coins have been issued in Canada at various times since 1858, often in official cases. A representative selection follows. Sets from 1908 are in leather or leatherette covered presentation cases.

Date	Description	Buying Price
1858	Victoria: 1, 5, 10, 20 cents	3,000.00
1870	Victoria: 5, 10, 25, 50 cents	8,000.00
1908	Edward VII: 1, 5, 10, 25, 50 cents	1,000.00
1911	George V: 1, 5, 10, 25, 50 cents	3,000.00
1937	George VI: 1, 5, 10, 25, 50 cents $1	500.00
1937	George VI: as above, but in card case	250.00
1967	Elizabeth II: Centennial, 1, 5, 10, 25, 50 cents $1.00, $20.00 gold	195.00
1967	Elizabeth II: Centennial, as above, but with medal instead of $20.00 gold	10.00

1976 MONTREAL OLYMPIC COINS

For the Summer Olympic Games of 1976, held in Montreal, seven series of silver coins were minted. There were four different coins in each series. Two $5.00 and two $10.00 coins, struck in sterling silver. The $5.00 coins weigh 24.4 grams and the $10.00 coins weigh 48.6 grams. The coins were available, encapsulated in plastic, as single coins, and in Custom, Prestige and Proof four coin sets. Each set of four coins, $30.00, contain 4.28 oz. of fine silver. The purchase price of these sets is linked to the market price of silver, even if the intrinsic value falls below the face value. Large quantities of these coins were issued and they are not redeemable by the government or the banks.

SERIES I

$5 Map of North America

$5 Kingston

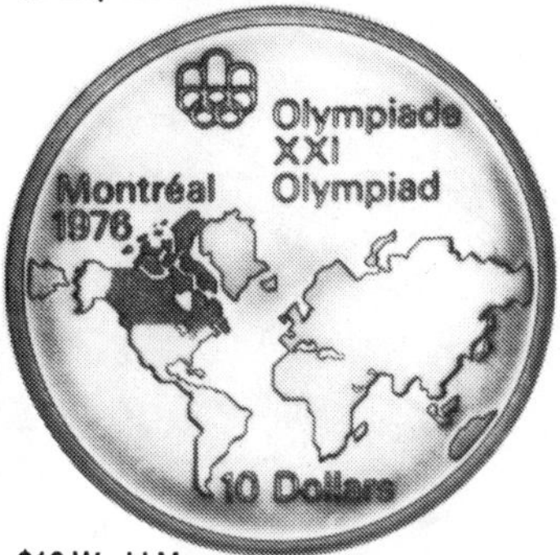

$10 World Map

$10 Montreal

SERIES II

$5 Athlete with Torch

$5 Olive Wreath

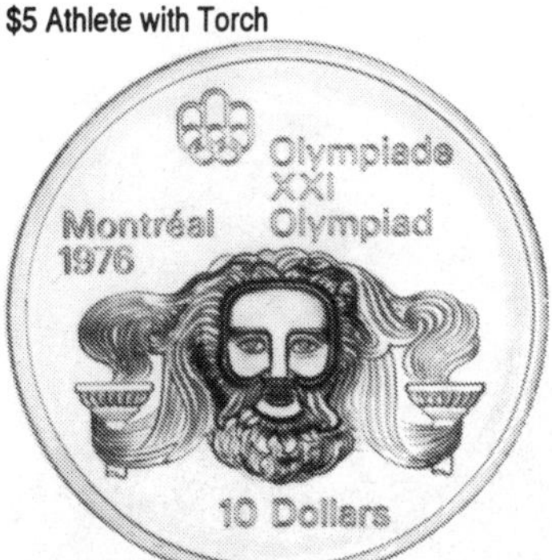

$10 Head of Zeus

$10 Temple of Zeus

SERIES III

$5 Canoeing

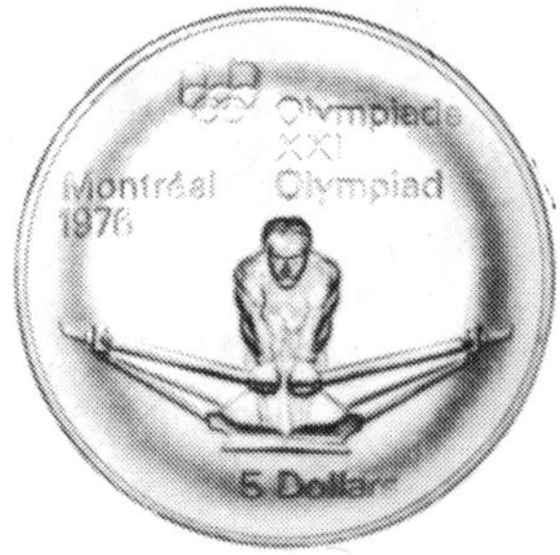

$5 Rowing

$10 Lacrosse

$10 Bicycling

SERIES IV

$5 The Marathon

$5 Ladies' Javelin

$10 Men's Hurdles

$10 Ladies' Shot Put

SERIES V

$5 The Diver

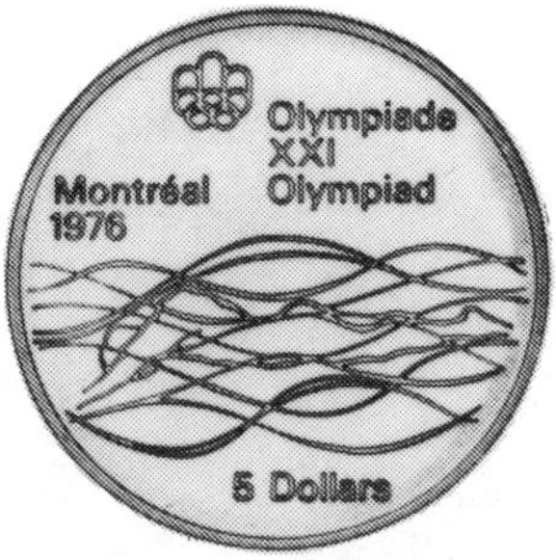

$5 The Swimmer

$10 The Paddler

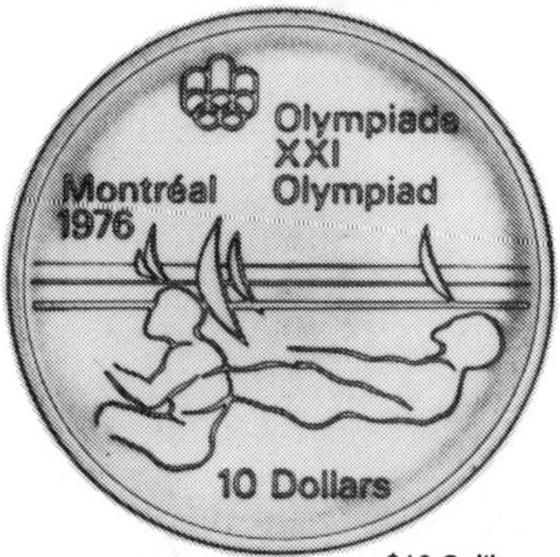

$10 Sailing

SERIES VI

$5 Fencing

$5 Boxing

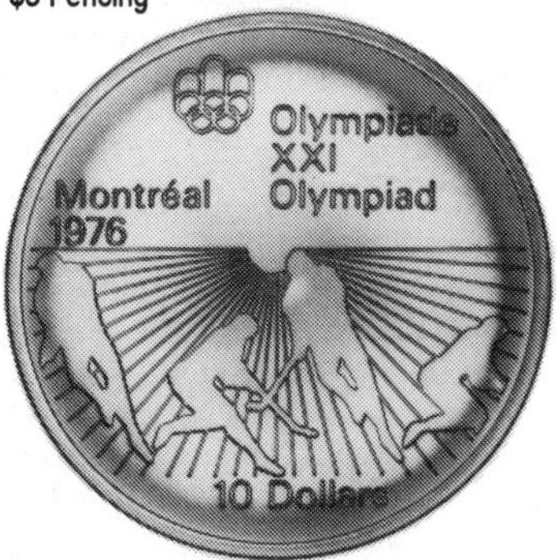

$10 Field Hockey

$10 Football

SERIES VII

$5 Olympic Village

$5 Olympic Flame

$10 Olympic Stadium

$10 Olympic Velodrome

Date	Series	$5 Coin	$10 Coin	Custom Set	Prestige Set	Proof Set
1973	1	5.00	10.00	30.00	30.00	32.50
1974 Mule			100.00			
1974	2	5.00	10.00	30.00	30.00	32.50
1974	3	5.00	10.00	30.00	30.00	32.50
1975	4	5.00	10.00	30.00	30.00	32.50
1975	5	5.00	10.00	30.00	30.00	32.50
1976	6	5.00	10.00	30.00	30.00	34.00
1976	7	5.00	10.00	30.00	30.00	35.00

1988 CALGARY OLYMPIC GAMES

The XV Winter Olympic Games were held in Calgary, February 13th to 29th, 1988. Ten different $20 silver coins were issued to commemorate this event. The coins weigh 34.107 grams, the composition is .925 silver and .075 copper, and they were issued in Proof-singles or Proof-Sets in one or two coin display cases. Incorporated into the design of these coins are the letters "XV OLYMPIC WINTER GAMES - XV es JEUX OLYMPIQUE D'HIVER" impressed into the edge. During the striking of these coins at the Royal Canadian Mint the impressed procedures were skipped on some series resulting in the edge lettering being missed on four known coins resulting in varieties.

FIRST SERIES

Downhill Skiing

Speed Skating

SECOND SERIES

Hockey

Biathalon

THIRD SERIES

Cross-Country Skiing

Free-Style Skiing

FOURTH SERIES

Figure Skating

Curling

FIFTH SERIES

Ski-Jumping

Bobsleigh

Date	Description	Proof Single	Proof Set
1985	Downhill Skiiing	20.00	
1985	Speed Skating	20.00	40.00
1985	Speed Skating, no edge lettering	100.00	
1986	Hockey	20.00	
1986	Hockey, no edge lettering	100.00	
1986	Biathalon	20.00	40.00
1986	Biathalon, no edge lettering	100.00	
1986	Cross-Country Skiing	20.00	
1986	Free-Style Skiing	20.00	40.00
1986	Free-Style Skiing, no edge lettering	100.00	
1987	Figure Skating	20.00	
1987	Curling	20.00	40.00
1987	Ski-Jumping	20.00	
1987	Bobsleigh	20.00	40.00

AVIATION TWENTY DOLLARS 1990 - 1994

Canada's Aviation heroes and achievements are commemorated on this series of twenty dollar sterling silver coins. The series will be made up of ten coins issued two per year over the next five years. For the first time, each coin design contains a 24 karat gold covered oval cameo portrait of the aviation hero commemorated.

A maximum of 50,000 of each coin will be offered for sale.

FIRST SERIES

Coin No. 1
Anson and Harvard/Leckie

Coin No. 2
Lancaster/Fauquier

SECOND ISSUE

Coin No. 3
A.E.A. Silver Dart/F.W. Baldwin,
John A. D. McCurdy

Coin No. 4
de Havilland Beaver/Phillip C. Garratt

THIRD ISSUE

Coin No. 5
Curtiss UN-4/Sir F.W. Baillie

Coin No. 6
de Havilland Beaver/Phillip C. Garratt

FOURTH ISSUE

Coin No. 7
Fairchild 71C/J.A.Richardson

Coin No. 8
Super Electra/Z.L.Leigh

Date	Description	PR-65
1990	Anson and Harvard/Leckie	25.00
1990	Lancaster/Fauquier	25.00
1991	Silver Dart/Baldwin, McCurdy	25.00
1991	Beaver/Garratt	25.00
1992	Curtiss/Baille	25.00
1992	Gypsy Moth/Seymour	25.00
1993	Faichild/Richardson	25.00
1993	Super Electra/Leigh	25.00

ONE HUNDRED DOLLARS

Canada issued the first one hundred dollar gold coin in 1976 to commemorate the Montreal Olympic Games. In that year two qualities and fineness were released; uncirculated - .585 fine (14 karat) and proof - .900 fine (22 karat). From 1976 to 1986 only proof quality coins with a fineness of .925 were issued. In 1987 the quality remained the same (proof) but the fineness of the coin was altered to .585 fine or 14 karat, again.

IMPORTANT

Proof coins must be in mint state condition. Mishandled, mounted or damaged coins are discounted from the prices listed. The buying price for gold coins is tied to the market price of gold. Any movement in the gold price will result in a corresponding price movement for these coins.

1976 - 14 kt

1976 - 22 kt

1977

1978

1979

1980

1981

1982

1983

1984

Date	Description	Fineness	Buying Price
1976	14 kt Olympic	.585	120.00
1976	22 kt Olympic	.900	240.00
1977	Jubilee	.925	240.00
1978	Unity	.925	240.00
1979	Year of the Child	.925	240.00
1980	Arctic Territories	.925	240.00
1981	"O" Canada	.925	240.00
1982	Constitution	.925	240.00
1983	Gilbert's Landing	.925	240.00
1984	Voyage of Discovery	.925	240.00

ONE HUNDRED DOLLARS

1985

1986

1987

1988

1989

1990

1991

1992

1993

1994

NOT
AVAILABLE
AT PRESSTIME

1995

Date	Description	Fineness	Buying Price
1985	National Parks	.925	240.00
1986	Peace	.925	240.00
1987	Winter Olympic Games	.585	110.00
1988	Bowhead Whale	.585	175.00
1989	Ste. Marie	.585	175.00

Date	Description	Fineness	Buying Price
1990	Literacy Year	.585	120.00
1991	Empress of India	.585	120.00
1992	Montreal	.585	120.00
1993	Horseless Carraige	.585	120.00
1994	The Home Front	.585	120.00
1995	Design Not Available	.585	120.00

TWO HUNDRED DOLLARS

1990

1991

1992

1993

1994

Date	Description	Fineness	Buying Price
1990	Canada Flag	.916	250.00
1991	A National Passion	.916	250.00
1992	Niagara Falls	.916	250.00
1993	RCMP	.916	250.00
1994	Anne of Green Gables	.916	250.00

MAPLE LEAF BULLION COINS

The Maple Leaf gold coins were first produced in 1979, the fractional or small sizes three years later in 1982 and the half ounce size in 1986. In 1988 platinum and silver coins were issued to complete the precious metal series.

The Maple Leaf bullion coins are purchased based on the spot market on the day of purchase times their gold content less a small handling charge.

$50

$20

$10

$5

PLATINUM AND GOLD CONTENTS

1/10 Maple Leaf	$5 - 0.10 troy ounce	1/2 Maple Leaf	$20 - 0.50 troy ounce
1/4 Maple Leaf	$10 - 0.25 troy ounce	Maple Leaf	$50 - 1.00 troy ounce

SILVER CONTENT

Maple Leaf	$5 - 1.00 troy ounce

MAPLE LEAF PROOF BULLION ISSUES OF 1989

To commemorate the 10th anniversary of the maple leaf bullion program the Royal Canadian Mint in 1989, issued a series of proof condition silver, gold and platinum coins individually and in sets. The single coins and sets were packaged in solid maple wood presentation cases with brown velvet liners.

Composition	Description	Market Price
Gold	Gold coin: 1 ounce maple	600.00
	Gold coin set, 4 coins: 1, 1/2, 1/4, 1/10 ounce maple	1,300.00
Platinum	Platinum coin set, 4 coins: 1, 1/2, 1/4, 1/4, 1/10 ounce maple	2,200.00
Silver	Silver coin: 1 ounce maple	70.00
Silver, Gold and Platinum	1 ounce coin set, 3 coins: 1 ounce maples of silver, gold and platinum	1,400.00
	Precious metal set, 3 coins: 1 ounce silver and 1/10 ounce maples of gold and platinum	200.00

PROOF PLATINUM COINS

In 1990 the Royal Canadian Mint entered the luxury market for high quality collector coins. Canada's "Monarch of the North" has been transferred from the sparkling Arctic environment by Robert Bateman to the gleaming surface of pure platinum coins.

1990 POLAR BEAR

1991 SNOWY OWL

1992 COUGAR

1993 ARTIC FOX

Date	Description	Buying Price
1990	Polar Bear - 4 coins: $300, $150, $75, $30	1000.00
1991	Snowy Owl - 4 coins: $300, $150, $75,$30	1000.00
1992	Cougar - 4 coins: $300, $150, $75, $30	1000.00
1993	Artic Fox - 4 coins: $300, $150, $75, $30	1000.00

PAPER MONEY OF CANADA

PROVINCE OF CANADA

1866 ISSUES

Denom.	Issue Date	Buying Price
$1	1866	100.00
$2	1866	400.00
$5	1866	600.00
$10	1866	800.00
$20	1866	1000.00
$50	1866	3000.00

DOMINION OF CANADA

1870 ISSUES

Denom.	Issue Date	Buying Price
25-cent Plain	1870	6.00
25-cent Series A	1870	20.00
25-cent Series B	1870	8.00

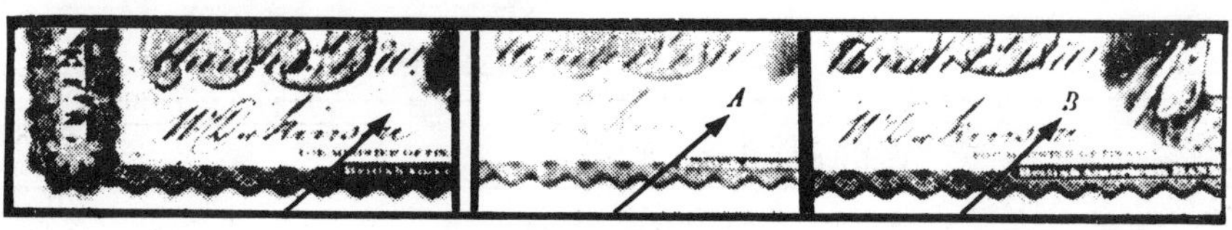

Plain Series Letter "A" Series Letter "B"

1870 ISSUES

Denom.	Issue Date	Variety/Signature	Buying Price
$1	1870	Payable at Montreal or Toronto	75.00
$1	1870	Payable at Halifax	300.00
$1	1870	Payable at St. John	300.00
$2	1870	Payable at Montreal or Toronto	450.00
$2	1870	Payable at Halifax or St. John	1300.00

1878 ISSUES

Denom.	Issue Date	Variety/Signature	Buying Price
$1	1878	Scalloped Frame, Payable at Montreal or Toronto	75.00
$1	1878	Scalloped Frame, Payable at St. John or Halifax	300.00
$1	1878	Lettered Frame, Payable at Montreal or Toronto	25.00
$1	1878	Lettered Frame, Payable at St. John or Halifax	200.00
$2	1878	Payable at Montreal or Toronto	200.00
$2	1878	Payable at St. John or Halifax	300.00

1882 AND 1887 ISSUES

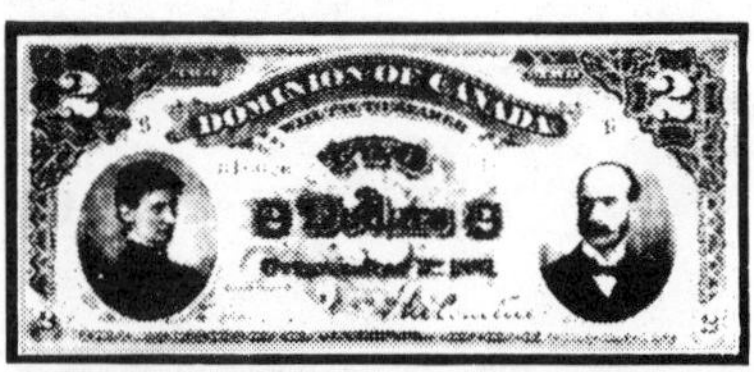

Denom.	Issue Date	Variety/Signature	Buying Price
$4	1882		150.00
$2	1887	Plain, Series A	60.00

1897 AND 1898 ISSUES

No "One"

Inward "One"

Outward "One"

Denom.	Issue Date	Variety/Signature	Buying Price
$1	1897	Green face tint	60.00
$2	1897	Red-brown back	150.00
$2	1897	Dark brown back	20.00
$1	1898	Inward "One"	20.00
$1	1898	Outward "One"	18.00

1900 AND 1902 ISSUES

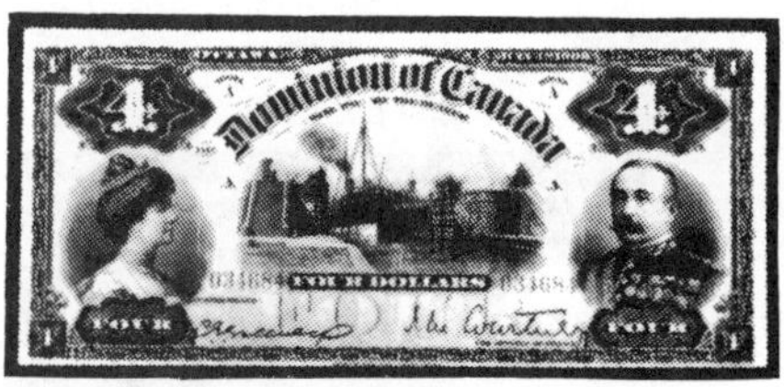

"4" on Top

"Four" on Top

Denom.	Issue Date	Variety/Signature	Buying Price
25-cent	1900	Courtney	3.00
25-cent	1900	Bouville	3.00
25-cent	1900	Saunders	3.00
$4	1900		80.00
$4	1902	"4" on Top	80.00
$4	1902	"Four" on Top	80.00

Note: All buying prices are for notes in very good condition.

1911 AND 1912 ISSUES

No Seal Seal over Five Seal Only

Denom.	Issue Date		Buying Price
$1	1911	Green Line/Black line series	10.00
$500	1911		2,000.00
$1,000	1911		2,500.00
$5	1912	No Seal	20.00
$5	1912	Seal over Five	30.00
$5	1912	Seal only	20.00

1914 AND 1917 ISSUES

Denom.	Issue Date	Variety/Signature	Buying Price
$2	1914	No Seal	15.00
$2	1914	Seal over Two	25.00
$2	1914	Seal only	20.00
$1	1917	No Seal	10.00
$1	1917	With Seal	15.00
$1	1917	Black Seal	15.00

1923 ISSUES

Denom.	Issue Date	Variety/Signature	Buying Price
25-cent	1923	Hyndman/Saunders	3.00
25-cent	1923	McCavour/Saunders	3.00
25-cent	1923	Campbell/Clark	3.00
$1	1923	Various colour seals	10.00
$1	1923	Purple seal	30.00
$2	1923	Various colour seals	10.00
$2	1923	Green seal	12.00
$2	1923	Bronze seal	12.00

1924 AND 1925 ISSUES

Denom.	Issue Date	Variety/Signature	Buying Price
$5	1924	Queen Mary	150.00
$500	1925	George V	1,500.00
$1,000	1925	Queen Mary	2,500.00

Note: All buying prices are for notes in very good condition.

BANK OF CANADA

1935 ISSUES

Denom.	Variety	Buying Price
$1	English text	5.00
$1	French text	5.00
$2	English text	10.00
$2	French text	10.00
$5	English text	15.00
$5	French text	15.00
$10	English text	20.00
$10	French text	25.00
$20	English text, small seal	50.00
$20	French text	50.00
$25	English text	150.00
$25	French text	200.00
$50	English text	100.00
$50	French text	100.00
$100	English text	110.00
$100	French text	120.00
$500	English and French	1000.00
$1,000	English and French	1,050.00

1937 ISSUES

IMPORTANT

Bank notes with tears, missing corners, pinholes or folding creases are not considered to be very fine (VF). Notes in poor condition are not collectable.

	Very Fine Buying Prices By Signature		
Denom.	Osborne	Gordon	Coyne
$1	4.00	3.00	3.00
$2	6.00	4.00	4.00
$5	25.00	6.00	6.00
$10	13.00	10.00	10.00
$20	30.00	20.00	20.00
$50	75.00	50.00	50.00
$100	110.00	100.00	100.00
$1,000	1,025.00	Not Issued	

1954 ISSUES

"DEVIL'S FACE" PORTRAIT

IMPORTANT

The buying prices listed below are for notes in extremely fine condition. The notes must be clean with no tears, pinholes or noticeable folds or creases.

THE DEVIL'S FACE NOTES

On the earliest notes of the 1954 issue, highlighted areas of the Queen's hair produced the illusion of a leering demonic face behind her ear. This was not the result of an error, nor was it, as some have asserted, the prank of an IRA sympathizer at the bank note company. It was merely the faithful reproduction of the original photograph. The portrait of the Queen with the "Devil's Face" outlined in her hair generated almost instant controversy.

ASTERISK NOTES

Asterisk notes are replacement notes. The first being spoiled in printing, cutting, etc., and replaced by an asterisk note.

	Very Fine Buying Price by Signature			
	Coyne/Towers		Beattie/Coyne	
Denom.	Regular	Asterisk	Regular	Asterisk
$1	3.00	75.00	2.00	50.00
$2	3.50	100.00	3.00	50.00
$5	7.00	200.00	7.00	110.00
$10	11.00	200.00	11.00	100.00
$20	25.00	200.00	20.00	150.00
$50	50.00	NI	50.00	NI
$100	100.00	NI	100.00	NI
$1,000	1,000.00	NI	NI	NI

*NI - Not Issued

MODIFIED PORTRAIT

IMPORTANT

The buying prices listed below are for notes in uncirculated condition (new). The note must be clean, crisp, with no tears, creases, folds or marks of any kind or description.

MODIFIED PORTRAIT

The portrait was modified by darkening the highlights in the hair and thus removing the shading which had resulted in the "devil". The modification of the face plates was made for most denominations in 1956, except for the $1,000 denomination which was modified several years later.

Uncirculated Buying Price by Signature

	Beattie/Coyne		Beattie/Rasminsky		Bouey/Raminsky		Lawson/Bouey	
Denom.	Regular	Astrisk	Regular	Asterisk	Regular	Asterisk	Regular	Asterisk
$1	1.75	10.00	1.75	3.00	1.75	3.00	1.75	2.00
$2	6.00	20.00	2.50	4.00	2.50	3.00	2.50	4.00
$5	10.00	20.00	7.50	10.00	10.00	15.00	NI	NI
$10	15.00	25.00	12.50	15.00	NI	NI	NI	NI
$20	30.00	40.00	25.00	40.00	NI	NI	NI	NI
$50	60.00	NI	55.00	NI	NI	NI	100.00	NI
$100	105.00	NI	105.00	NI	NI	NI	105.00	NI
$1,000	1,000.00	NI	1,000.00	NI	1,000.00	NI	1,000.00	NI

*NI - Not Issued

$1 CENTENNIAL 1967

For the centennial of Canada's Confederation a special $1 note was issued. The note has a single design and two types of serial numbers, regular serial numbers and a special number "1867 - 1967". The special series was available from the Bank of Canada as a collector's item, but examples were soon found in circulation. In addition there was an asterisk note series for replacement notes.

Denom.	Issue Date	Variety	Uncirculated Buying Price
$1	1967	Commemorative serial number 1867-1967	1.00
$1	1967	Regular serial number	1.00
$1	1967	Asterisk Serial Number	1.50

1969 - 1975 ISSUE

This new series combined fine line engraving with subtle variations to make notes that are extremely difficult to counterfeit. The series features a new portrait of the Queen as well as portraits of previous prime ministers of Canada.

IMPORTANT

The buying prices listed on the following page are for notes in uncirculated condition (new). The note must be clean, crisp, with no tears, creases, folds or marks of any kind or description.

1969-1975 ISSUES

ASTERISK REPLACEMENT NOTES

Replacement of defective notes by asterisk notes was continued when the 1968-1975 issue was introduced. The highest denomination of the 1954 issue to be printed with asterisks was the $20; however, all denominations in the 1969-1975 issue including the $50 and $100 notes occur with asterisks in front of the two letter prefix type.

When the triple letter prefix notes were introduced in 1981, the use of asterisk notes was discontinued. For triple letter prefix notes, a replacement note is designated by the use of an "X" for the third letter.

Asterisk Notes
BC-46aA

"X" Replacement Notes
BC-46A-i

	Uncirculated Buying Price by Signature							
	Beattie/Rasminsky		Bouey/Rasminsky		Lawson/Bouey		Crow/Bouey	
Denom.	Regular	Asterisk	Regular	Asterisk	Regular	Asterisk	Regular	Asterisk
$1	NI	NI	NI	NI	1.25	1.50	1.00	1.50
$2	NI	NI	NI	NI	2.25	4.00	2.00	20.00
$5	NI	NI	7.50	10.00	7.00	8.00	NI	NI
$10	15.00	20.00	20.00	15.00	12.00	15.00	12.00	15.00
$20	22.00	25.00	NI	NI	22.00	25.00	NI	NI
$50	NI	NI	NI	NI	50.00	60.00	50.00	55.00
$100	NI	NI	NI	NI	100.00	105.00	100.00	105.00

Note: The Thiessen/Crow combination of signatures does not command a numismatic premium at this time.

*NI - Not Issued

1979 ISSUES

The series beginning in 1979 is a modification of the previous issue. The face designs are similar, as is the colouration. The serial numbers are moved to the back of the note at the bottom where the name of the Bank of Canada previously appeared. The black serial numbers are machine readable.

IMPORTANT

The buying prices listed below are for notes in uncirculated condition (new). The note must be clean, crisp, with no tears, creases, folds or marks of any kind or description.

REPLACEMENT NOTES

There are no asterisk notes in this issue. The replacement notes are designated by the second digit in the serial number.

The digit 1 following the first digit 3 of the $5 notes designates a replacement note. In the $20 denomination the replacement notes can be distinguished by "510" for the CBN company and "516" for the BABN company.

$5 Replacement Note

$20 Replacement Note

	Uncirculated Buying Price by Signature					
	Lawson/Bouey		Crow/Bouey		Thiessen/Crow	
Denom.	Regular	Asterisk	Regular	Astrisk	Reguar	Asterisk
$5	6.00	30.00	6.00	60.00	NI	NI
$20	25.00	30.00	20.00	25.00	20.00	25.00

1986 ISSUES

On March 14, 1986, the Bank of Canada introduced a new series of bank notes. The new designs were launched that year with the issue of the $2 and $5 notes. The Bank of Canada has not undertaken a redesign of the $1 note due to the Government of Canada's decision to introduce the one-dollar coin for circulation. The $1 note was phased out at the beginning of 1989.

Notes from 1986 to date do not command a numismatic premium above face value.

NEWFOUNDLAND PUBLIC WORKS CASH NOTES

Denom.	Buying Price
40-cents	35.00
50-cents	35.00
80-cents	40.00
$1	50.00
$5	75.00

Denom.	Buying Price
25-cents	10.00
50-cents	10.00
$1	20.00
$2	50.00
$5	100.00

GOVERNMENT NOTES

Denom.	Buying Price
$1	8.00
$2	12.00

PRINCE EDWARD ISLAND

Denom.	Buying Price
1848-1870 £1	250.00
1872 $10	200.00
1872 $20	200.00

NOVA SCOTIA

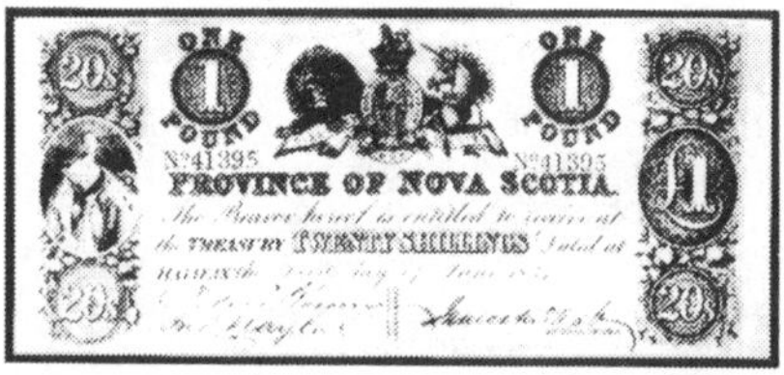

Denom.	Buying Price
1848-1854 £1	75.00
1861 $5	100.00

CANADIAN NOTE-ISSUING BANKS

The following list of banks identifies in alphabetical order all the non-government banks which issued or ordered Canadian notes.

Bank notes were first issued in Canada in 1813 and continued until 1943. One hundred and sixty different banks issued notes and some over a long period of time. There are literally thousands of different notes and if you add different grades, the number rises to tens of thousands. Far beyond the scope of this guide.

If you have a bank note that is on this list of banks then it is Canadian and please check with your local coin dealer for current buying prices.

The Bank of Acadia, Liverpool, N.S., 1872-1873
The Accommodation Bank, Kingston, U.C., 1836-1837
The Agricultural Bank, Montreal, L.C. 1837,
The Agricultural Bank, Toronto, U.C. 1834-1837
Arman's Bank, Montreal, L.C., 1837
Barclay's Bank (Canada), Montreal, Que., 1929-1956
La Banque du Boucherville, Boucherville, L.C., 1830's
The Bank of Brantford, Brantford, C.W., 1857-1860's
The British Canadian Bank, Toronto, Ont., 1883-1884
The Bank of British Columbia, Victoria, B.C., 1862-1901
The Bank of British North America, 1836-1918
Canada Bank, Montreal, L.C., 1792
The Canada Bank, Toronto, C.W., 1855
The Bank of Canada, Montreal, L.C., 1813-1831
The Canadian Bank of Commerce, Toronto,Ont., 1867-1961
Banque Canadienne, St. Hyacinthe, L.C., 1836-1838
Banque Canadienne Nationale, Montreal, Que., 1924-1979
The Central Bank of Canada, Toronto, Ont., 1883-1887
Central Bank of New Brunswick, Fredericton, N.B., 1834-1866
Charlotte County Bank, St. Andrew's, N.B., 1825-1865
Bank of Charlottetown, Charlottetown, P.E.I., 1852
The City Bank, Montreal, L.C., 1833-1876
City Bank, Saint John, N.B., 1836-1839
The Bank of Clifton, C.W., 1859-1863
The Colonial Bank of Canada, Toronto, C.W., 1856-1863
The Colonial Bank of Chatham, Chatham, U.C., 1837-1839
Commercial Bank, Brockville, U.C., 1837
Commerical Bank, Kingston, U.C., 1837
The Commercial Bank of Canada, Kingston, C.W., 1856-1868
The Commercial Bank of Fort Erie, Fort Erie, U.C., 1836-1839
The Commercial Bank of Lake Ontario, Niagara Falls, U.C., 1837
The Commercial Bank of Manitoba, Winnipeg, Man., 1885-1893
The Commercial Bank of the Midland District, Kingston, U.C., 1831-1856
Commercial Bank of Montreal, Montreal, L.C., 1835-1837
Commercial Bank of New Brunswick, Saint John, N.B., 1834-1868
The Commercial Bank of Newfoundland, St. John's Nfld., 1857-1894
Commercial Bank of Windsor, Windsor, N.S., 1864-1902
Commercial Branch Bank of Canada, Collingwood, C.W., 1861-1879
The Consolidated Bank of Canada, Montreal, Que., 1876-1879
The Bank of the County of Elgin, St. Thomas, C.W., 1857-1862
The Crown Bank of Canada, Toronto, Ont., 1904-1908
The Dominion Bank, Toronto, Ont., 1869-1955
Eastern Bank of Canada, Saint John, N.B., 1928-1934
The Eastern Townships Bank, Sherbrooke, C.E., 1855-1912
The Exchange Bank, Quebec, L.C., 1840's
The Exchange Bank of Canada, Montreal, Que., 1871-1883

The Exchange Bank of Canada, Windsor, Ont., 1860's
The Exchange Bank of Toronto, C.W., 1855
The Exchange Bank of Yarmouth, Yarmouth, N.S., 1867-1903
The Exchange Bank Company of Chippewa, Chippewa, U.C., 1837
The Farmer's Bank, Toronto, U.C., 1840's
The Farmers Bank of Canada, Toronto, Ont., 1906-1910
The Farmer's Bank of Malden, Malden, U.C., 1840's
The Farmer's Joint Stock Banking Co., Toronto, U.C., 1835-1849
The Farmers J.S. Banking Co., Toronto, U.C., 1830's
The Farmers Bank of Rustico, Rustico, P.E.I., 1862-1892
The Farmers Bank of St. John's, St. John's, L.C., 1837-1838
The Federal Bank of Canada, Toronto, Ont., 1874-1888
The Bank of Fredericton, Fredericton, N.B., 1836-1839
The Free Holders Bank of the Midland District, Bath, U.C., 1837
Goderich Bank, Goderich, U.C., 1834
The Gore Bank, Hamilton, U.C., 1835-1870
The Gore Bank of Hamilton, Hamilton, U.C., ca. 1837
The Grenville County Bank, Prescott, C.W., 1856
The Halifax Banking Company, Halifax, N.S., 1825-1903
The Hamilton Bank, Hamilton, L.C., 1835
The Bank of Hamilton, Hamilton, Ont. 1872-1923
Hart's Bank, Three Rivers, L.C., 1835-1847
Henry's Bank, La Prairie and Montreal, L.C., 1837
Banque d'Hochelaga, Montreal, Que., 1873-1925
The Home Bank of Canada, Toronto, Ont., 1903-1923
The Bank of Hull, Hull, L.C., 1837
The Imperial Bank of Canada, Toronto, Ont., 1873-1961
The International Bank of Canada, Toronto, U.C., 1858-1859
Banque Internationale du Canada, Montreal, Que., 1911-1913
La Banque Jacques Cartier, Montreal, C.E., 1861-1900
The Kingston Bank, Kingston, L.C., 1837
The Bank of Liverpool, Liverpool, N.S., 1871-1879
The Bank of London in Canada, London, Ont., 1883-1888
Lower Canada Bank, Montreal, L.C., 1837
The Bank of Lower Canada, Quebec, L.C., late 1830's MacDonald & Co., Victoria, B.C., 1859-1866
The Maritime Bank of the Dominion of Canada, Saint John, N.B., 1872-1887
The Mechanics Bank, Montreal, L.C., 1837
The Mechanics Bank, Montreal, C.E., 1865-1879
The Mechanics Bank of Saint John's, Saint John's, L.C., 1837
The Merchantile Banking Corporation, Halifax, N.S., 1878
The Merchants Bank, Montreal, C.E., 1864-1868
The Merchants Bank, Toronto, U.C., 1837
The Merchants Bank of Canada, Montreal, Que., 1868-1923
The Merchants Bank of Halifax, Halifax, N.S., 1864-1901
The Merchants Bank of Prince Edward Island, Charlottetown, P.E.I., 1871-1906
The Merchants Exchange Bank, Goderich, C.W., 1853
The Metropolitan Bank, Montreal, Que., 1871-1876
The Metropolitan Bank, Toronto., 1902-1914
The Molsons Bank, Montreal, C.E., 1837-1925
Montreal Bank, Montreal, L.C., 1817-1822
The Montreal Bank, Montreal, C.W., 1840's-1850's
The Bank of Montreal, Montreal, L.C., 1822 to date
La Banque Nationale, Montreal, C.E., 1860-1925
The Bank of New Brunswick, Saint John, N.B. 1820-1913
The Newcastle Banking Co., Amherst, U.C., 1836
The Newcastle District Loan Company, Peterborough, U.C., 1836

The Newcastle District Bank, St. Catharines, C.W., 1853-1875
The Niagara Suspension Bridge Bank, Queenston, U.C., 1836-1841
The Northern Bank, Winnipeg, Man., 1905-1908
The Northern Crown Bank, Winnipeg, Man., 1908-1918
The Bank of Nova Scotia, Halifax, N.S., 1832 to date
The Ontario Bank, Bowmanvile, C.W., 1857-1906
The Bank of Ottawa, Montreal, L.C., 1837
The Bank of Ottawa, Ottawa, Ont., 1874-1919
The Bank of the People, Toronto, U.C., 1835-1841
La Banque du Peuple, Montreal,, L.C., 1835-1895
The People's Bank of Halifax, Halifax, N.S., 1864-1905
The People's Bank of New Brunswick, Fredericton, N.B., 1864-1907
The Pheonix Bank, Phillipsburg, L.C., 1837-1841
The Pictou Bank, Pictou, N.S., 1873-1887
The Bank of Prince Edward Island, Charlottetown, P.E.I., 1856-1881
The Provincial Bank, London, Ont., 1884
The Provincial Bank of Canada, Stanstead, Ont., 1856-1863
La Banque Provinciale du Canada, Montreal, Quec., 1900-1979
The Quebec Bank, Quebec, L.C., 1818-1917
Bank of Quebec Lower Canada, Quebec, L.C., 1841
The Royal Bank of Canada, Montreal, Que., 1901 to date
The Royal Canadian Bank, Toronto, C.W., 1864-1876
The Saint Francis Bank, Stanstead, C.E., 1855
La Banque de St. Hyacinthe, St. Hycainthe, Que., 1873-1908
La Banque de St. Jean, St. Jean, Que., 1873-1908
Banque St. Jean Baptiste, Montreal, Que., 1875
The St. Lawrence Bank, Toronto, Ont., 1872-1876
The St. Lawrence Bank & Lumber Co., Malbaie, L.C., 1837
The St. Stephen's Bank, St. Stephen, N.B., 1836-1910
The Bank of Saskatchewan, Moose Jaw, Sask., 1913
The Sovereign Bank of Canada, Montreal, Que., 1901-1908
The Stadacona Bank, Quebec City, Que., 1872-1879
The Standard Bank of Canada, Toronto, Ont., 1876-1928
The Sterling Bank of Canada, Toronto, Ont., 1905-1924
The Summerside Bank, Summerside, P.E.I., 1866-1901
Tattersall Bank, Montreal, L.C., 183-
The Bank of Toronto, Toronto, Ont., 1855-1954
The Traders Bank of Canada, Toronto, Ont., 1885-1912
The Union Bank, Montreal, L.C., 1838-ca 1840
The Union Bank of Canada, Quebec City, Que., 1886-1925
The Union Bank of Halifax, Halifax, N.S., 1856-1910
The Union Bank of Lower Canada, Quebec, C.E., 1865-1886
The Union Bank of Montreal, Montreal, L.C., ca 1840
Union Bank of Newfoundland, St. John's, Nfld., 1854-1894
The Union Bank of Prince Edward Island, Charlottetown, P.E.I., 1860-1893
United Empire Bank of Canada, Toronto, Ont., 1906-1911
Bank of Upper Canada, Kingston, U.C., 1819-1822
Bank of Upper Canada, York, U.C., 1821-1866
The Bank of Vancouver, Vancouver, B.C., 1910-1914
The Bank of Victoria, Victoria, U.C., 1836
La Banque Ville Marie, Montreal, Que., 1872-1899|
The Bank of Western Canada, Clifton, C.W., 1859-1863
The Western Bank of Canada, Oshawa, Ont., 1882-1909
The Westmoreland Bank of New Brunswick, N.B., 1854-1867
The Weyburn Security Bank, Weyburn, Sask., 1910-1931
The Bank of Yarmouth, Yarmouth, N.S., 1859-1905
The Zimmerman Bank, Elgin, C.W., 1854-1859

COLONIAL COINS AND TOKENS

Canada has produced a great number of tokens of various kinds over the years. Tokens were used as a form of currency prior to the institution of the decimal currency system in 1858 (Colonial issues are not all tokens, some being regal coins). After Confederation, other kinds of tokens appeared, such as those for services, transportation and advertising purposes.

The prices in this section are for tokens in V.G. (Very Good) or F. (Fine) condition. Higher prices will be paid for rare issues or for tokens in V.F. (Very Fine) or better condition.

NEWFOUNDLAND TOKENS

Date and Description	Buying Price
Rutherford - St. John's	2.00
Rutherford - Harbour Grace	2.00
McAuslane	600.00

Date and Description	Buying Price
1858 Sailing Ship	80.00
1860 Fishery Rights	12.00

PRINCE EDWARD ISLAND TOKENS

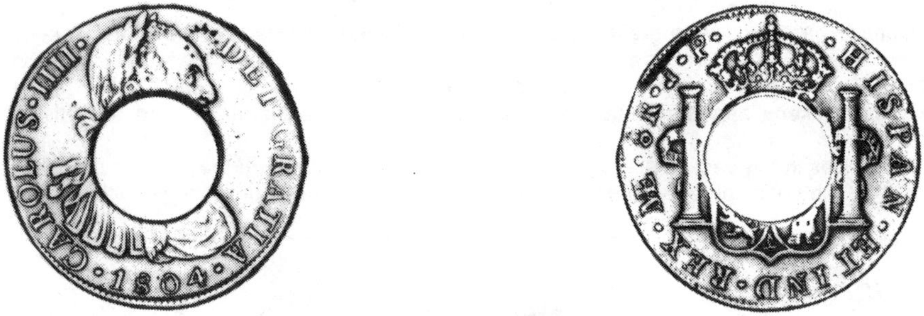

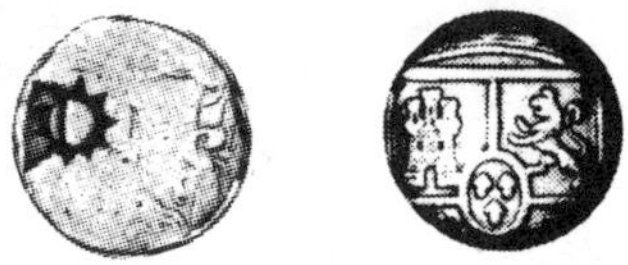

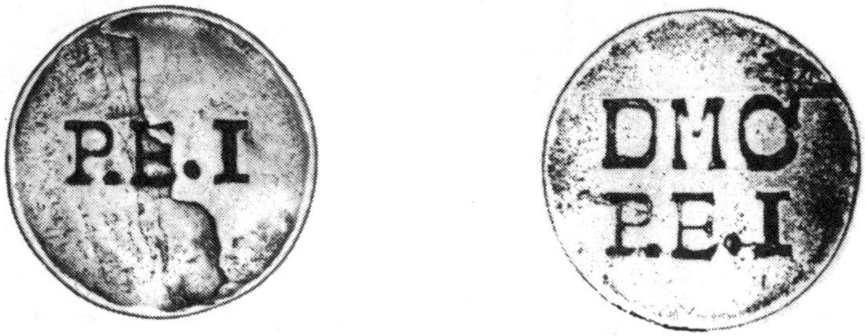

Date and Description	Buying Price	Date and Description	Buying Price
Holey Dollar Ring*	1,100.00	McCarthy Penny	550.00
Holey Dollar Plug*	1,100.00	Sheaf of Wheat	125.00
McCausland Penny	550.00	Speed The Plough	1.50

Note: Forgeries exist and are worth considerably less.

PRINCE EDWARD ISLAND TOKENS

Date and Description	Buying Price
Fisheries & Agriculture	1.50
Self Government 1855 Prince Edward's	1.50
Self Government 1855 Prince Edward	1.50
Self Government 1857	1.50
Fisheries & Agriculture	1.50
Ships Colonies 1815 One Penny	6.00
Ships Colonies 1815 Publick Accommodation	6.00
Ships Colonies	1.50

NOVA SCOTIA
SEMI-REGAL TOKENS

Date and Description	Buying Price	Date and Description	Buying Price
1823 Halfpenny	.50	1840 Halfpenny	.50
1823 Penny	1.00	1840 Penny	1.00
1824 Halfpenny	.50	1843 Half Penny	.50
1824 Penny	1.00	1843 Penny	1.00
1832 Halfpenny	.50	1856 Halfpenny	.50
1832 Penny	1.00	1856 Penny	1.00

NOVA SCOTIA
PRIVATE TOKENS

Date and Description	Buying Price
Broke - Halifax	2.00
Convenience of Trade	3.00
Carritt & Alport	3.00
Hosterman & Etter	2.00
Hosterman & Etter 1815	2.00
Starr & Shannon	1.00
Commercial Change	1.00
Miles W. White	1.00

NOVA SCOTIA
PRIVATE TOKENS

Date and Description	Buying Price
John Alexr Barry	1.00
Halifax Nova Scotia	2.00
W. A. & S. Black's	2.00
J. Brown	1.00
W. L. White's	10.00
Trade & Navigation 1812	1.00
Trade & Navigation 1813	10.00
Pure Copper Preferable	1.00
Success to Navigation	1.00
N.S & N.B. Success	10.00

NEW BRUNSWICK TOKENS

Date and Description	Buying Price
1843 Halfpenny	.50
1843 Penny	.75
1854 Halfpenny	.50
1854 Penny	.75

Date and Description	Buying Price
McDermott	150.00
St. John	2.00
St. John's	1,000.00

LOWER CANADA TOKENS

Date and Description	Buying Price
Magdalen Island	10.00
Bank Token	1.00
Banque Du Peuple, Maple Leaf	1.00
Banque Du Peuple, Wreath	1.00

Date and Description	Buying Price
Pro Bono Publico	1,000.00
Bank Token Halfpenny	.75
Bank Token Penny	1.00
Bank of Montreal	
Sideview Halfpenny	200.00
Sideview Penny	400.00

LOWER CANADA TOKENS

Date and Description	Buying Price
Montreal Half Penny	2.00
Canada Half Penny	2.00
For Public Accommodation	2.00
T.S. Brown & Co.	2.00
Ths & Wm Molson	75.00

Date and Description	Buying Price
Francis Mullins & Son	3.00
R.W. Owen	500.00
J. Shaw & Co.	3.00
J. Roy	15.00
Agriculture & Commerce	.75

LOWER CANADA TOKENS

Date and Description	Buying Price
Halfpenny Token 1812, Small Wreath	1.00
Halfpenny Token 1812, Large Wreath	1.00
Penny Token 1812	2.00
Victoria Nobis Est	2.00
R H Half Penny	2.00

Date and Description	Buying Price
To Facilitate Trade	
Military Bust 1825	2.00
Civilian Bust 1825	500.00
Spread Eagle	1.00
Halfpenny Token	2.00

LOWER CANADA TOKENS

Date and Description	Buying Price
Seated Justice	1.00
Bust/Ships Colonies	1.00

Date and Description	Buying Price
Commercial Change	2.00
Bust and Harp	1.00

WELLINGTON TOKENS

Date and Description	Buying Price
Field Marshal Wellington	1.00
Marquis Wellington	2.00

Date and Description	Buying Price
The Illustrious Wellington	1.00
Battle Token	1.00

UPPER CANADA TOKENS

Date and Description	Buying Price
Copper Company	100.00
Lesslie Halfpenny	2.00
Lesslie Twopenny	20.00
No Labour No Bread	.75
Sir Isaac Brock	.75

Date and Description	Buying Price
Success To Commerce	1.00
Upper & Lower Canada	15.00
Commercial Change 1815	10.00
Commerical Change 1820	1.00

UPPER CANADA TOKENS

Date and Description	Buying Price
Commercial Change 1821	
Cask Marked Upper Canada	10.00
Cask Marked Jamaica	200.00
Province of Upper Canada	5.00

Date and Description	Buying Price
To Facilitate Trade	
1823	2.00
1833	1.00
Commercial Change 1833	2.00

PROVINCE OF CANADA TOKENS

PROVINCE OF CANADA TOKENS

Date and Description	Buying Price
Bank of Montreal 1837-1845	
1842, 1844 Halfpenny	.50
1845 Halfpenny	1,000.00
1837 Penny	50.00
1842 Penny	1.00
Quebec Bank 1852	
Halfpenny	.50
Penny	1.00
Bank of Upper Canada 1850-1857	
Halfpenny	.50
Penny	1.00

ANONYMOUS AND MISCELLANEOUS TOKENS

Date and Description	Buying Price
For General Accommodation	1.00
Success to Trade	10.00
Pure Copper Preferable	1.00
North American	10.00

BRITISH COLUMBIA TOKENS

Date and Description	Buying Price
1802 Pattern Gold $10	Very Rare
1802 Pattern Gold $20	Very Rare

NORTH WEST COMPANY

Date and Description	Buying Price
1820 North West Company Token	100.00

HUDSON'S BAY COMPANY

Date and Description	Buying Price
Hudson's Bay Company Tokens Set of four (1, 1/2, 1/4, 1/8)	30.00

TRANSPORTATION TOKENS

Date and Description	Buying Price
Bridge Tokens, each	40.00
Montreal & Lachine Railroad	20.00

CANADIAN MEDALS

WAR MEDALS 1812 TO 1885

Army Gold Cross

Naval General Service Medal

Army Gold Medal

Canadian General Service Medal

Army General Service Medal

Egyptian Medal

Date and Description	Buying Price
Army Gold Cross	10,000.00
Army Gold Medal	4,000.00
Army General Service Medal 1812-1814	
Fort Detroit Bar	1,500.00
Chateauguay Bar	1,500.00
Chrysler's Farm Bar	1,500.00
Naval General Service Medal 1812-1814	150.00

Date and Description	Buying Price
Canadian General Service Medal	
Fenian Raid Bar 1866	100.00
Fenian Raid Bar 1870	110.00
Red River Bar 1870	500.00
Egyptian Medal*	
The Nile Bar	500.00
Kirbekan Bar	500.00

*Awarded to Canadian Boatmen

WAR MEDALS 1885 TO 1914

Khedive's Bronze Star

1914 Star

North West Canada Medal

1914-1915 Star

South Africa Medal

British War Medal

Date and Description	Buying Price
Khedive's Bronze Star	15.00
North West Canada Medal 1885	150.00
Saskatchewan Bar	200.00
Queen's South Africa	
1899-1900 on reverse	1,500.00
Dates removed	15.00
King's South Africa	15.00

Date and Description	Buying Price
1914 Star*	500.00
1914-1915 Star	5.00
British War Medal	8.00

*Canadian Star awarded to 2nd. Field Hospital only.

WAR MEDALS 1914 TO 1945

Allied Victory Medal

The Defence Medal

Merchantile Marine War Medal

WW II 1939-1945 War Medal

Canadian Volunteer Service Medal

Atlantic
Air Crew Europe
Africa
France and Germany
Italy
Pacific
Burma

Date and Description	Buying Price
Allied Victory Medal	2.00
Merchantile Marine War Medal	5.00
Canadian Volunteer Service Medal	8.00
Defence Medal	8.00
1939-1945 War Medal	8.00

Date and Description	Buying Price
1939-1945 Star	2.00
Atlantic Star	10.00
Air Crew Europe	50.00
Africa Star	2.00
France and Germany Star	2.00
Italy Star	2.00
Pacific Star	6.00
Burma Star	6.00

WAR MEDALS
1951 TO 1973

Canadian
Korean
Medal

United
Nations
Korea
Medal

United
Nations
Emergency
Medal

Date and Description	Buying Price
Canadian Korean War Medal, English	20.00
Canadian Korean War Medal, French	30.00
United Nations Korea Medal	10.00
United Nations Emergency Medal	10.00
United Nations Medal 1960 to present	10.00
International Commission Medal 1967	10.00
International Commission Medal 1973	10.00

COMMEMMORATIVE MEDALS

1911
Coronation
Medal

1935
Silver
Jubilee
Medal

1937
Coronation
Medal

Date and Description	Buying Price
King George V	
Coronation Medal - 1911	15.00
Silver Jubilee Medal - 1935	12.00
King George VI	
Coronation Medal - 1937	12.00

COMMEMORATIVE MEDALS

1953
Coronation
Medal

1977
Silver
Jubilee
Medal

1967
Canadian
Centennial
Medal

Date and Description	Buying Price
Queen Elizabeth II	
Coronation Medal - 1953	10.00
Silver Jubilee Medal - 1977	35.00
Canadian Centennial Medal - 1967	25.00

MEDALS FOR VALOUR AND SERVICE

Victoria
Cross

Distin-
guished
Service
Order

Order of
St. Michael
and
St. George

Date and Description	Buying Price
Victoria Cross	10,000.00
Distinguished Service Order	200.00
Order of St. Michael and St. George	200.00

MEDALS FOR VALOUR AND SERVICE

Distin-
guished
Service
Cross

Air
Force
Medal

Distin-
guished
Flying
Cross

Military
Medal

Air Force
Cross

British
Empire
Medal

Date and Description	Buying Price
Distinguished Service Cross	200.00
Distinguished Flying Cross	225.00
Air Force Cross	275.00

Date and Description	Buying Price
Air Force Medal	100.00
Military Medal	150.00
British Empire Medal	50.00

COINS OF THE UNITED STATES

MINT MARKS

The United State decimal coinage is identified by the following mint marks:

- C -Charlotte, North Carolina
- CC -Carson City, Nevada
- D -Dahlonega, Georgia (gold coins only)
- D -Denver, Colorado (1906 to date)
- O -New Orleans, Louisiana
- S -San Francisco, California
- P -Philadelphia, Pennsylvania

HALF CENTS

Liberty Cap

Date and Mint Mark	Buying Price
1793	700.00
1794	100.00
1795	110.00
1796	1,350.00
1797	110.00

Draped Bust

Date and Mint Mark	Buying Price
1800	15.00
1802	200.00
1803-1808	12.00

Classic Head

Date and Mint Mark	Buying Price
1809-1810	15.00
1811	75.00
1825 to 1835	15.00

Braided Hair

Date and Mint Mark	Buying Price
1849 to 1857	15.00

IMPORTANT

Do not clean your coins. Coins should be handled carefully. Only experts should consider cleaning. If you are not an expert the results can be disastrous.

LARGE CENTS

Flowing Hair

Date and Mint Mark	Buying Price
1793	1000.00

Liberty Cap

Date and Mint Mark	Buying Price
1793	500.00
1794	75.00
1795	80.00
1796	75.00

Draped Bust

Date and Mint Mark	Buying Price
1796	30.00
1797	20.00
1798	15.00
1799	400.00
1800 to 1803	15.00
1804	50.00
1805 to 1807	10.00

Classic Head

Date and Mint Mark	Buying Price
1808	15.00
1809	25.00
1810	10.00
1811	20.00
1812 to 1814	10.00

Coronet Head

Date and Mint Mark	Buying Price
1816 to 1820	5.00
1821	4.00
1822	3.00
1823	8.00
1824 to 1838	3.00
1839 to 1856	3.00
1857	4.00

SMALL CENTS

Flying Eagle

Date and Mint Mark	Buying Price
1856	750.00
1857 to 1858	5.00

Indian Head

Date and Mint Mark	Buying Price
1859 to 1865	1.00
1866 to 1868	5.00
1869 to 1872	7.00
1873 to 1876	1.00
1877	50.00
1878 to 1886	.25
1887 to 1908	.20
1908S	4.00
1909	.20
1909S	25.00

Lincoln Head Wheat Ears

Date and Mint Mark	Buying Price
1909	.03
1909VDB	.10
1909S	5.00
1909SVDB	50.00
1910 to 1914	.03
1914D	10.00
1915D to 1931D	.02
1931S	5.00
1932 to 1954	.01

Lincoln Head Memorial

Date and Mint Mark	Buying Price
1955 Double Date	20.00
1955 to 1992	.01

TWO CENTS

Date and Mint Mark	Buying Price
1864 to 1871	2.00
1872	20.00
1873 Proof	500.00

THREE CENTS

Silver

Date and Mint Mark	Buying Price
1851 to 1862	5.00
1863 to 1873 Proof	300.00

Nickel

Date and Mint Mark	Buying Price
1865 to 1874	2.00
1875 to 1876	3.00
1877 to 1878 Proof	250.00
1879 to 1880	15.00
1881	1.00
1882	15.00
1883	30.00
1884 to 1887	100.00
1888 to 1889	15.00

FIVE CENTS NICKEL

Shield

Date and Mint Mark	Buying Price
1866 to 1876	3.00
1879 to 1881	50.00
1882 to 1883	3.00

Liberty Head

Date and Mint Mark	Buying Price
1883 to 1884	1.00
1885	60.00
1886	20.00
1887 to 1912	.25
1912S	7.00

Indian Head or Buffalo Type

Date and Mint Mark	Buying Price
1913	1.00
1914 to 1918	.10
1918D 8/7	100.00
1919 to 1938	.10

Jefferson Type

Date and Mint Mark	Buying Price
1938 to 1992	.05

HALF DIMES

Flowing Hair

Date and Mint Mark	Buying Price
1794	250.00
1795	150.00

Draped Bust

Date and Mint Mark	Buying Price
1796 to 1797	250.00
1800 to 1801	200.00
1802	2,000.00
1803 to 1805	175.00

Capped Bust

Date and Mint Mark	Buying Price
1829 to 1837	5.00

Liberty Seated

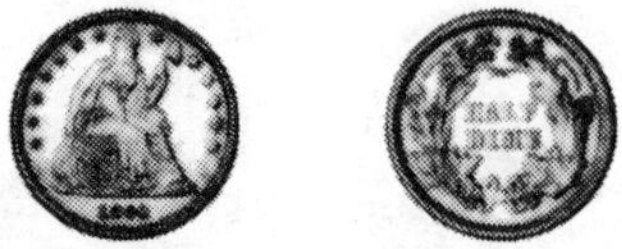

Date and Mint Mark	Buying Price
1837	10.00
1838 No Stars	20.00
1838 to 1845	2.00
1846	50.00
1847 to 1863	2.00
1864	75.00
1864S	5.00
1865	60.00
1866	50.00
1866S	4.00
1867	75.00
1867S	4.00
1868 to 1873	2.00

DIMES

Draped Bust

Date and Mint Mark	Buying Price
1796 to 1979	400.00
1798 to 1807	200.00

Capped Bust

Date and Mint Mark	Buying Price
1809 to 1811	25.00
1814 to 1821	6.00
1822	75.00
1823 to 1837	5.00

Liberty Seated

Date and Mint Mark	Buying Price
1837 to 1838	7.00
1839 to 1843	3.00
1843O and 1844	20.00
1845	3.00
1846	30.00
1847 to 1856	3.00
1856S	25.00
1857 to 1860	3.00
1858S	25.00
1859S	25.00
1860O	150.00
1861 and 1862	3.00
1863	30.00
1864 to 1867	35.00
1864S to 1867S	4.00
1868 to 1874	3.00
1871CC	100.00
1872CC	60.00
1873CC	125.00
1874CC	150.00
1875 to 1878	2.00
1878CC	3.00
1879	17.00
1880 to 1881	15.00
1882 to 1885	2.00
1885S	17.00
1886 to 1891	2.00

Barber

Date and Mint Mark	Buying Price
1892 to 1895	2.00
1895O	50.00
1896O	12.00
1897 to 1916	.50

Mercury Head

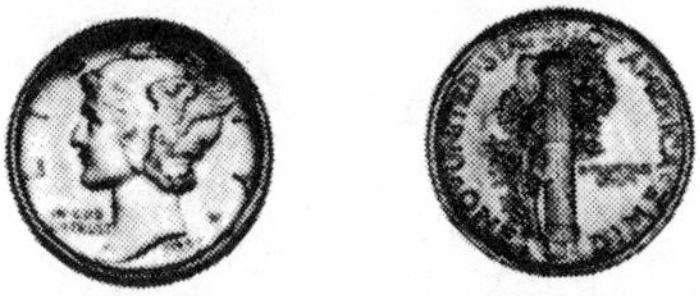

Date and Mint Mark	Buying Price
1916	.35
1916D	100.00
1917 to 1945	.35

Roosevelt - Silver

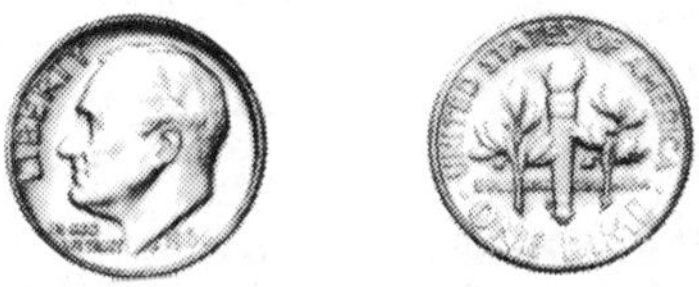

Date and Mint Mark	Buying Price
1946 to 1964	.35

Roosevelt - Clad

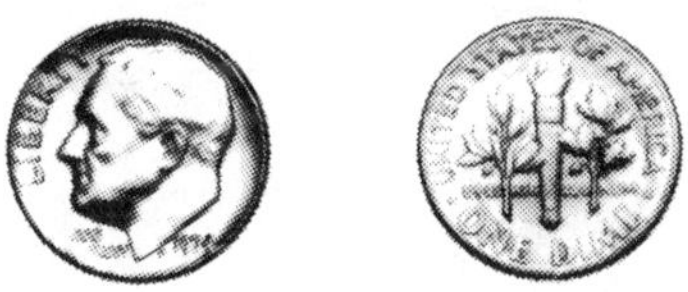

Date and Mint Mark	Buying Price
1965 to 1992	.10

TWENTY CENTS

Date and Mint Mark	Buying Price
1875 to 1876	20.00
1877 to 1878 Proof	1,000.00

QUARTER DOLLAR

Draped Bust

Date and Mint Mark	Buying Price
1796	1,500.00
1804	300.00
1805 to 1807	75.00

Capped Bust

Date and Mint Mark	Buying Price
1815 to 1822	20.00
1823	1,500.00
1824 to 1838	20.00

Liberty Seated

Date and Mint Mark	Buying Price
1838 to 1849	4.00
1849O	100.00
1850 to 1851	4.00
1851O	50.00
1852	5.00
1852O	75.00

Date and Mint Mark	Buying Price
1853 No Arrows	50.00
1853 to 1873	5.00
1870CC	400.00
1871CC	200.00
1871S	60.00
1872CC	80.00
1874 to 1878	3.00
1879 to 1888	25.00
1889 to 1891	3.50

Barber

Date and Mint Mark	Buying Price
1892 to 1896	1.50
1896S	60.00
1897 to 1901	1.50
1901S	400.00
1902 to 1913	1.50
1913S	100.00
1914 to 1916	1.50

Standing Liberty

Date and Mint Mark	Buying Price
1916	300.00
1917 to 1930	.90

Note: Coins must be in very good condition or better to command these prices, coins grading good or less will sell at lower prices.

Washington - Silver

Date and Mint Mark	Buying Price
1932 to 1964	.90

Washington - Clad

Date and Mint Mark	Buying Price
1965 to 1975	.25

200th Bi-Centennial

Date and Mint Mark	Buying Price
1976	.25

Washington - Clad

Date and Mint Mark	Buying Price
1977 to 1992	.25

HALF DOLLARS

Flowing Hair

Date and Mint Mark	Buying Price
1794	300.00
1795	175.00

Draped Bust

Date and Mint Mark	Buying Price
1796 15 Stars	3,500.00
1796 16 Stars	3,500.00
1797 15 Stars	3,500.00
1801 to 1802	75.00
1803 to 1807	60.00

Capped Bust

Date and Mint Mark	Buying Price
1807	15.00
1808 to 1814	7.00
1815	200.00
1817 to 1836	10.00
1836 Reeded Edge	175.00
1837 to 1839	10.00
1839O	40.00

Liberty Seated

Date and Mint Mark	Buying Price
1839 to 1852	10.00
1850	20.00
1851	20.00
1852	35.00
1852O	10.00
1853 to 1855	6.00
1855S Arrows	100.00
1856 to 1878	6.00
1870CC	175.00
1871CC to 1878CC	15.00
1878S	1500.00
1879 to 1890	50.00
1891	7.00

Barber

Date and Mint Mark	Buying Price
1892	6.00
1892O and 1892S	30.00
1893 to 1897	3.00
1897O	15.00
1897S	20.00
1898 to 1915	2.50

Liberty Walking

Date and Mint Mark	Buying Price
1916 to 1920	1.80
1921	15.00
1921D	20.00
1923 to 1947	1.80

Franklin

Date and Mint Mark	Buying Price
1948 to 1963	1.80

Kennedy - Silver

Date and Mint Mark	Buying Price
1964	1.80

Kennedy - Silver Clad

Date and Mint Mark	Buying Price
1965 to 1970	.55

Kennedy - Copper Clad

Date and Mint Mark	Buying Price
1971 to 1992	.50

SILVER DOLLARS

Flowing Hair

Date and Mint Mark	Buying Price
1794	2,500.00
1795	400.00

Draped Bust

Date and Mint Mark	Buying Price
1795	300.00
1796 to 1798	250.00
1798 to 1803	125.00

Note: Coins must grade very good (VG) or better to command prices listed.

Liberty Seated

Date and Mint Mark	Buying Price
1840 to 1873	50.00
1851	600.00
1870CC	80.00
1870S	12,500.00
1871CC	600.00
1872CC	175.00
1872S	75.00
1873CC	750.00

Liberty Head

Date and Mint Mark	Buying Price
1878 to 1892	5.00
1879CC and 1881CC	25.00
1882CC and 1884CC	10.00
1885CC	40.00
1889CC	80.00
1893CC	30.00
1893O	25.00
1893S	400.00
1894	100.00
1895O	25.00
1895S	40.00
1896 to 1903	5.00
1903O	40.00
1904 to 1921	5.00

Peace

Date and Mint Mark	Buying Price
1921 to 1927	5.00
1928	30.00
1928S to 1935	5.00

Eisenhower

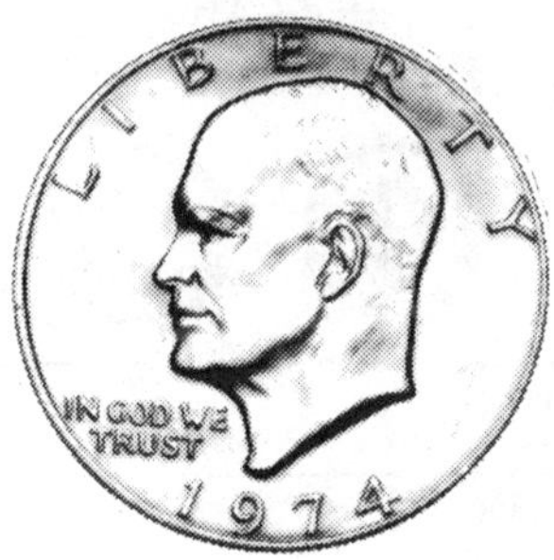

Date and Mint Mark	Buying Price
1971 to 1976	1.00

Susan B. Anthony

Date and Mint Mark	Buying Price
1979 to 1981	1.00

TRADE DOLLARS

Date and Mint Mark	Buying Price
1873 to 1878	25.00
1878CC	40.00

GOLD COINS

DOLLARS
Type 1 Liberty Head

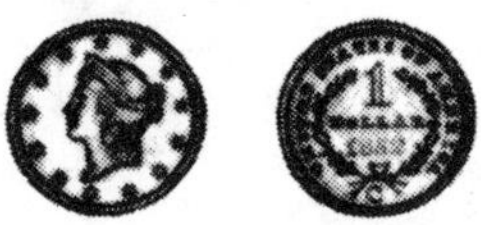

Date and Mint Mark	Buying Price
1849 to 1854	75.00

Type 2 Indian Head Small

Date and Mint Mark	Buying Price
1854 to 1855	125.00
1855C	300.00
1855D	700.00

Type 3 Indian Head Large

Date and Mint Mark	Buying Price
1856 to 1889	75.00
1856D	600.00
1860D	500.00
1861D	2,000.00
1875	500.00

QUARTER EAGLES (2 1/2 DOLLARS)

Capped Bust Right

Date and Mint Mark	Buying Price
1796	2,000.00
1797 to 1807	600.00

Capped Bust Left

Date and Mint Mark	Buying Price
1808	3,000.00

Capped Head Left

Date and Mint Mark	Buying Price
1821 to 1827	600.00
1829 to 1833	500.00
1834	1,300.00

Classic Head

Date and Mint Mark	Buying Price
1834 to 1839	80.00

Coronet Head

Date and Mint Mark	Buying Price
1840 to 1907	80.00
1848 California	1,500.00
1854D	500.00
1854S	5,000.00
1855D	600.00
1856D	800.00
1875	450.00

Indian Head

Date and Mint Mark	Buying Price
1908 to 1929	80.00
1911D	200.00

3 DOLLARS

Date and Mint Mark	Buying Price
1854 to 1873	250.00
1854D	1,500.00
1873 Closed 3	600.00
1880 to 1889	275.00

4 DOLLARS

Date and Mint Mark	Buying Price
1879 to 1880	5,000.00

HALF EAGLES (5 DOLLARS)

Capped Bust Right

Date and Mint Mark	Buying Price
1795 to 1797	1,500.00
1798 to 1807	500.00

Draped Bust Left

Date and Mint Mark	Buying Price
1807 to 1834	500.00
1821	800.00
1822	50,000.00
1823	800.00
1824	1,600.00
1825	900.00
1826	1,000.00
1827	1,600.00
1828	1,600.00
1829	5,500.00

Classic Head

Date and Mint Mark	Buying Price
1834 to 1838	100.00
1838C	200.00
1838D	200.00

Coronet Head

Date and Mint Mark	Buying Price
1839 to 1908	90.00
1842C Small Date	175.00
1854S	5,000.00
1861C	300.00
1861D	1,000.00
1864S	175.00
1865	150.00
1870CC	300.00
1875	3,000.00
1878CC	200.00

Indian Head

Date and Mint Mark	Buying Price
1908 to 1916	125.00
1929	650.00

EAGLE (10 DOLLARS)

Capped Bust Right

Date and Mint Mark	Buying Price
Small Eagle, 1795 to 1797	1,500.00
Heraldic Eagle, 1797 to 1803	500.00

Coronet Head

Date and Mint Mark	Buying Price
1838 to 1907	200.00
1858	1,000.00
1859O	300.00
1859S	225.00
1863	500.00
1864S	450.00
1865S	225.00
1866S	225.00
1870CC	300.00
1873	350.00
1873CC	225.00
1875 Proof	8,000.00
1876	275.00
1877	300.00
1877CC	225.00
1878CC	225.00
1879CC	500.00
1879O	300.00
1883O	450.00

$10 Indian Head

Date and Mint Mark	Buying Price
1907 to 1932	250.00
1920S	1,100.00
1930S	650.00
1933	10,000.00

DOUBLE EAGLES ($20 DOLLARS)

Liberty

Date and Mint Mark	Buying Price
1849 to 1907	450.00
1854O	7,000.00
1855O	800.00
1856O	7,000.00
1859O	500.00
1860O	500.00
1861O	450.00
1870CC	3,000.00
1871CC	500.00
1879O	500.00
1881	500.00
1882	800.00
1885	600.00
1886	1,00.00
1891	500.00
1891CC	500.00

$20 St. Gaudens

Date and Mint Mark	Buying Price
1907 MCMVII	850.00
1907 to 1916	450.00
1920S	1,500.00
1921	2,500.00
1922 to 1928	450.00
1927D	50,000.00
1927S	750.00
1929	750.00
1930 to 1932	1,250.00

GOLD COMMEMORATIVE COINS

Date and Mint Mark	Buying Price
1903 $1 Louisiana Purchase, Jefferson	150.00
1903 $1 Louisiana Purchase, McKinley	150.00
1904 $1 Louis & Clark Exposition	175.00
1905 $1 Louis & Clark Exposition	175.00
1915S $1 Panama-Pacific Exposition	140.00
1916 $1 McKinley Memorial	140.00
1917 $1 McKinley Memorial	140.00
1922 $1 Grant Memorial, With Star	400.00
1922 $1 Grant Memorial, Without Star	500.00
1915S $2.50 Panama-Pacific Exposition	350.00
1926 $2.50 Philadelphia Sesquicentennial	150.00
1984P $10 Olympic	210.00
1984D $10 Olympic	205.00
1984S $10 Olympic	200.00
1984W $10 Olympic	200.00
1986W $5 Liberty	90.00
1987W $5 Constitution	80.00
1988W $5 Oylmpic	85.00
1989W $5 Congress	85.00
1991W $5 Mount Rushmore	90.00
1992W $5 Olympic	90.00
1992W $5 Columbus	120.00
1993W $5 Bill of Rights	110.00
1993W $5 WWII	100.00
1994W $5 World Cup	100.00

WORLD GOLD COINS

This partial listing of world gold coins indicates the prices dealers are willing to pay based on the Canadian dollar gold price as at June 3rd, 1994. Prices **will** fluctuate with the market price of gold plus the Canadian/U.S. dollar exchange rate.

AUSTRIA

Date and Denom.	Fine Gold Content oz	Buying Price
1912 10K	0.0980	41.00
1915 20K	0.1960	82.00
1915 100K	0.9803	410.00
1915 1D	0.1109	47.00
1914 4D	0.4438	188.00
1892 10Fr	0.0933	39.00
1892 20Fr*	0.1867	78.00

BAHAMAS

Date and Denom.	Fine Gold Content oz	Buying Price
1967 $10	0.1177	50.00
1971 $10	0.1177	50.00
1972 $10	0.0940	40.00
1967 $20	0.2355	100.00
1971 $20*	0.2355	100.00
1972 $20	0.1880	80.00
1967 $50	0.5888	250.00
1971 $50	0.5888	250.00
1972 $50	0.4708	198.00
1967 $100	1.1776	500.00
1971 $100	1.1776	500.00
1972 $100	0.9420	395.00

* Coin illustrated

BELGIUM

Date and Denom.	Fine Gold Content oz	Buying Price
1867 to 1914 20Fr	0.1867	78.00

BERMUDA

Date and Denom.	Fine Gold Content oz	Buying Price
1970 $20	0.2355	98.00
1977 $50	0.1172	49.00
1975 $100*	0.2304	97.00
1977 $100	0.2344	100.00

CAYMAN ISLANDS

Date and Denom.	Fine Gold Content oz	Buying Price
1972 $25*	0.2532	107.00
1974 $50	0.1823	77.00
1974 $100	0.3646	154.00
1975 $100	0.3646	154.00
1977 $100	0.3464	146.00

CHILE

Date and Denom.	Fine Gold Content oz	Buying Price
1898 to 1900 5p	0.0883	37.00
1896 to 1901 10p*	0.1766	74.00
1896 to 1917 20p	0.3532	138.00
1926 to 1980 100p	0.5886	250.00

COLUMBIA

Date and Denom.	Fine Gold Content oz	Buying Price
1913 to 1929 2 1/2p	0.1177	50.00
1913 to 1930 5p	0.2355	100.00
1919 and 1924 10p	0.4710	200.00
1973 1500p*	0.5527	235.00

FRANCE

Date and Denom.	Fine Gold Content oz	Buying Price
1856 to 1869 5Fr	0.0467	20.00
1854 to 1914 10Fr	0.0933	40.00
1809 to 1914 20Fr*	0.1867	80.00
1810 to 1838 40Fr	0.3734	160.00
1855 to 1864 50Fr	0.4667	200.00
1855 to 1913 100Fr	0.9335	400.00

GERMANY

Date and Denom.	Fine Gold Content oz	Buying Price
1872 to 1914 10DM	0.1152	49.00
1871 to 1914 20DM*	0.2304	98.00

GREAT BRITAIN

Date and Denom.	Fine Gold Content oz	Buying Price
1863 to 1915 1/2 Sov.	0.1177	44.00
1871 to 1968 Sov.*	0.2354	97.00
1887 Two Pound	0.4708	250.00
1897 Two Pound	0.4708	250.00
1902 Two Pound	0.4708	250.00
1911 Two Pound	0.4708	250.00
1937 Two Pound	0.4708	250.00
1887 Five Pound	1.1773	550.00
1897 Five Pound	1.1773	550.00
1902 Five Pound	1.1773	550.00
1911 Five Pound	1.1773	550.00
1937 Five Pound	1.1773	550.00

IRAN

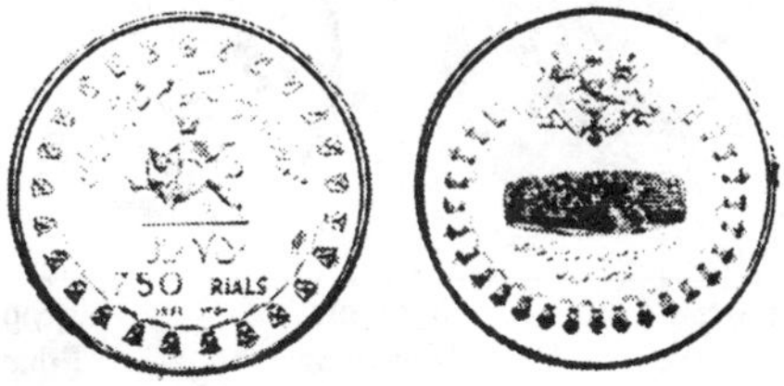

Date and Denom.	Fine Gold Content oz	Buying Price
1971 500R	0.1883	80.00
1971 750R*	0.2827	120.00
1971 1000R	0.3770	160.00
1971 2000R	0.7541	320.00

ITALY

Date and Denom.	Fine Gold Content oz	Buying Price
1932 to 1860 10L	0.0931	40.00
1831 to 1860 20L*	0.1866	80.00
1822 to 1831 40L	0.3733	160.00
1832 to 1844 100L	0.9332	400.00

JAMAICA

Date and Denom.	Fine Gold Content oz	Buying Price
1972 $20*	0.2531	107.00
1975, 1976 $100	0.2265	96.00
1978 $100	0.3281	140.00
1978, 1979 $250	1.2507	525.00

MEXICO

Date and Denom.	Fine Gold Content oz	Buying Price
1945 2p	0.0482	20.00
1945 2 1/2p	0.0602	25.00
1955 5p	0.1205	50.00
1959 10p*	0.2411	100.00
1959 20p	0.4823	200.00
1947 50p	1.2057	500.00

Above dates are restrikes.

NETHERLANDS

Date and Denom.	Fine Gold Content oz	Buying Price
1900 to 1937 1D*	0.1109	47.00
1912 5G	0.0973	41.00
1875 to 1933 10G	0.1947	82.00

PANAMA

Date and Denom.	Fine Gold Content oz	Buying Price
1975 to 1979 100B*	0.2361	100.00
1975 to 1979 500B	1.2067	510.00

RUSSIA

Date and Denom.	Fine Gold Content oz	Buying Price
1897 to 1911 5R*	0.1244	52.00
1897 7 1/2R	0.1867	79.00
1898 to 1911 10R	0.2489	104.00
1897 15R	0.3734	158.00
1977 to 1988 100R	0.5000	210.00

IMPORTANT

Buying prices are listed for coins graded VF or better. Bent, damaged or badly worn coins are worth less.

*Coin Illustrated

APPENDIX - BULLION VALUES

Silver and gold coins and other numismatic items are often bought by dealers for their bullion value, that is the value of the pure precious metals which they contain. The weight of precious metals is expressed in grams or troy ounces, not in avoirdupois ounces. A troy ounce is greater than an avoirdupois ounce.

1 Troy Ounce = 31.103 Grams
1 Avoirdupois Ounce = 28.349 Grams

GOLD

The quantity of pure gold in gold coins is calculated by multiplying the gold fineness or purity of the coin by its weight in troy ounces or grams. Gold purity can also be expressed in karats, a 24-part system with 24-karats equalling pure gold, 22 karats equalling 22 parts gold to 2 parts base metal, 18 karats equalling 18 part gold to 6 parts base metal etc.

Karats	Fineness	Purity
24	.999	99.9%
22	.916	91.6%
18	.750	75.0%
14	.585	58.5%
10	.417	41.7%
9	.375	37.5%

A 14-karat or .585 fine gold coin weighing 1 troy ounce contains 1 ounce x .585 = .585 troy ounces of pure gold. If gold is worth $600 per troy ounce, then this coin is worth $600 x .585 = $351. (See extended charts on following pages.)

SILVER

The quantity of pure silver in silver coins is calculated by multiplying the silver fineness or purity of the coin by its weight in troy ounces.

Karat	Fineness	Purity
Pure	.999	99.9%
Fine	.999	99.9%
Sterling	.925	92.5%
Coin	.800	80.0%
Coin	.500	50.0%

A .800 fine silver coin weighing 1 troy ounce contains 1 x .800 = .800 troy ounces or pure silver. If silver is worth $20 and ounce, then this coin is worth $20 x .800 = $16. (See extended charts on following pages.)

GOLD CONTENT OF CANADIAN GOLD COINS

Denom.	Date and Mint Mark	Gross Weight (Grams)	Fineness	Pure Gold Content Grams	Pure Gold Content Troy Oz.
NEWFOUNDLAND					
$2	1865-1888	3.33	.917	3.05	.100
CANADA					
1 pd.	1908C-1910C	7.99	.917	7.32	.236
1 pd.	1911C-1919C	7.99	.917	7.32	.236
$5	1912-1914	8.36	.900	7.52	.242
$10	1912-1914	16.72	.900	15.05	.484
$20	1967	18.27	.900	16.45	.529
$5 M.L.	1982 to Date	3.11	.9999	3.11	.10
$10 M.L.	1982 to Date	7.78	.9999	7.78	.25
$20 M.L.	1986 to Date	15.57	.9999	15.57	.500
$50 M.L.	1979 to Date	31.10	.999	31.10	1.000
$100	1976 (Unc.)	13.33	.583	7.78	.250
$100	1976 (Proof)	16.96	.917	15.55	.499
$100	1977-1986	16.96	.917	15.55	.499
$100	1987 to Date	13.33	.583	7.78	.250

SILVER CONTENT OF CANADIAN SILVER COINS

Denom.	Date	Fineness	Silver Content Grams	Silver Content Troy Oz.
$20	1985-1988	.925	31.103	1.000
$10	1973-1976	.925	44.955	1.445
$5	1973-1976	.925	22.477	.723
$5 M.L.	1987 to Date	.999	31.103	1.000
$1	1935-1967	.800	18.661	.600
$1	1971 to Date	.500	11.662	.375
50-cents	1870-1919	.925	10.792	.347
50-cents	1920-1967	.800	9.330	.300
25-cents	1870-1919	.925	5.370	.173
25-cents	1920-1967	.800	4.665	.150
25-cents	1967-1968	.500	2.923	.094
10-cents	1858-1919	.925	2.146	.069
10-cents	1920-1967	.800	1.866	.060
10-cents	1967-1968	.500	1.170	.038
5-cents	1858-1919	.925	1.080	.034
5-cents	1920-1921	.800	.933	.030

BULLION VALUES OF CANADIAN GOLD COINS

Computed from $300 to $700 per troy ounce in increments of $100 Canadian.

Denomination	Date and Mint Mark	$300	$400	$500	$600	$700
NEWFOUNDLAND						
$2	1865-1888	30.00	40.00	50.00	60.00	70.00
CANADA						
1 pd.	1908C-1910C	70.95	94.40	118.00	141.60	165.20
1 pd.	1911C-1919C	70.95	94.40	118.00	141.60	165.20
$ 5	1912-1914	72.60	96.80	121.00	145.20	160.40
$10	1912-1914	145.20	193.60	242.00	290.40	338.00
$20	1967	158.70	211.60	264.50	317.40	370.30
$5 M.L.	1982 to Date	30.00	40.00	50.00	60.00	70.00
$10 M.L.	1982 to Date	75.00	100.00	125.00	150.00	175.00
$20 M.L.	1986 to Date	150.00	200.00	250.00	300.00	350.00
$50 M.L.	1979 to Date	300.00	400.00	500.00	600.00	700.00
$100	1976 (Unc.)	75.00	100.00	125.00	150.00	175.00
$100	1976 (Pf)	150.00	200.00	250.00	300.00	350.00
$100	1977-1986	150.00	200.00	250.00	300.00	350.00
$100	1987 (Pf)	75.00	100.00	125.00	150.00	175.00

BULLION VALUES OF CANADIAN SILVER COINS

Computed from $5 to $50 per troy ounce in increments of $10 Canadian.

Denom.	Fineness	$5	$10	$20	$30	$40	$50
$20	.925	5.00	10.00	20.00	30.00	40.00	50.00
$10	.925	7.23	14.00	28.90	43.35	57.80	72.15
$5	.925	3.62	7.23	14.46	21.69	28.92	36.15
$5 M.L.	.999	5.00	10.00	20.00	30.00	40.00	50.00
$1	.800	3.00	6.00	12.00	18.00	24.00	30.00
$1	.500	1.88	3.75	7.50	11.25	15.00	18.75
50-cents	.925	1.74	3.47	6.94	10.41	13.88	17.35
50-cents	.800	1.50	3.00	6.00	9.00	12.00	15.00
25-cents	.925	.87	1.73	3.46	5.19	6.92	8.65
25-cents	.800	.75	1.50	3.00	4.50	6.00	7.50
25-cents	.500	.47	.94	1.88	2.82	3.76	4.70
10-cents	.925	.35	.69	1.38	2.07	2.76	3.45
10-cents	.800	.30	.60	1.20	1.80	2.40	3.00
10-cents	.500	.19	.38	.76	1.14	1.52	1.90
5-cents	.925	.17	.34	.68	1.02	1.36	1.70
5-cents	.800	.15	.30	.60	.90	1.20	1.50